The

FRMA
MANTRA

The Secret Life-Changing Success Code That 99.9% Are Not Aware!

Ratnesh Jain

ISBN 979-8-89233-934-6

CONTENTS

FOREWORD

Are you tired of feeling stuck, even though you know you're capable of achieving so much more? Success is within reach, and this book will show you exactly how to claim it.

When I first met Ratnesh Jain, it was clear he wasn't just a man of ideas—he was a man of action. Over the years, Ratnesh has built a reputation as a mentor, advisor, master dealmaker, an executive recruiter, and a transformational leader. He sees beyond challenges and identifies pathways to success with clarity and focus. But what truly sets him apart is his unwavering belief in one simple, yet powerful principle: **Focused, Rapid, Massive Action (FRMA)**.

In today's fast-paced, ever-changing world, so many people are trapped in cycles of over-analysis, self-doubt, and fear of failure. They attend countless seminars, read stacks of books, and take courses that promise to be "the secret" to their success. And yet, they still find themselves stuck—unable to take those decisive steps that will propel them toward their dreams. Ratnesh understands this struggle intimately, and that's exactly why this book is so powerful.

The stories within these pages aren't just inspiring—they're real. They're stories of people who faced adversity, felt uncertain, and didn't know their next move, yet chose to embrace the FRMA mantra. This single shift empowered them to change their lives in ways they never thought possible. Ratnesh's experience as a mentor and advisor shines through in every chapter, illustrating that success isn't about luck or waiting for the perfect moment. Success is about taking **focused, rapid, and massive action**, even when the odds seem stacked against you.

For those ready to break free from indecision, fear, or stagnation, this book will be a game-changer. It's a roadmap for anyone who is serious about achieving their biggest goals. I have personally witnessed the power of FRMA in my own journey, and I can confidently say this approach works. It's rooted in action, accountability, and an unshakeable commitment to growth.

If you're ready to transform your life, unleash your potential, and achieve your biggest dreams, Ratnesh's book will guide you every step of the way. The blueprint is here—all you have to do is take action.

Harsh G

Successful Entrepreneur/Business Leader

ACKNOWLEDGMENTS

This book, *The FRMA Mantra*, would not have been possible without the support, guidance, and encouragement of some incredible people in my life.

I extend my heartfelt gratitude to **Sakshi, Shivani, and Vithika** for helping me shape my thoughts and finalize this book. Your insights and feedback have been invaluable. (They helped me come back after scrapping 3 versions of this book).

A special thanks to my **biggest support system – my wife, Anita**, whose unwavering belief in me fuels my journey.

To my **critics and strongest allies in decision-making – Gautam, Vastuka, and Rishabh** – your perspectives have sharpened my vision and helped me stay grounded.

A huge shout-out to **my incredible team at BGR**, who stand by me every day, turning ideas into reality and making things happen with dedication and passion.

I am deeply grateful to the **10 big achievers** who generously shared their time, journeys, and invaluable insights. Their stories form the very core of this book, bringing the *FRMA Mantra* to life with real-world impact.

A special acknowledgment to **my own big personal and professional failures**—each setback has been a stepping stone, shaping my understanding of success and resilience. And to the **thousands of mentees** whose struggles, aspirations, and transformations have enriched my perspective. Their journeys have been my greatest learning ground.

Above all, **nothing would have been possible without the blessings of my late parents and gurus.** Their teachings continue to guide me in every step of life.

With deepest gratitude,

Ratnesh Jain

"Don't wait. The time will never be just right."

– Napoleon Hill

ABOUT THE AUTHOR

Ratnesh Jain is a transformational leader, master dealmaker, executive recruiter, mentor, and advisor to countless entrepreneurs and professionals worldwide. Over the decades, Ratnesh has earned a reputation for his keen insights, strategic thinking, and relentless focus on results. Known as a dealmaker and growth architect, he has helped clients build high-performing teams, drive business growth, and overcome seemingly insurmountable challenges.

Ratnesh's journey from multiple failures, determined business leader to a master mentor was shaped by his commitment to Focused, Rapid, Massive Action (FRMA). This principle, born from his years of real-world experience, has empowered him and his clients and mentees to consistently break through barriers and reach new levels of success. Ratnesh believes that success is not just reserved for the exceptionally talented but for those willing to take decisive, bold action.

As a mentor and advocate of action-oriented leadership, Ratnesh has guided leaders across diverse industries—banking, fintech, consumer, healthcare, manufacturing, emerging technology, and beyond—helping them unlock their full potential and execute with precision. His profound understanding of what "Not to do" and what drives success has made him a sought-after advisor and a beacon of inspiration for those aiming to create meaningful change in their careers and lives.

Beyond his professional work, Ratnesh is dedicated to sharing his wisdom and experience with a global audience. Through his writing, public speaking, and one-on-one mentoring, he has impacted countless individuals who aspire to lead and live with purpose.

Ratnesh's message is simple yet powerful:

"Success is not for the chosen few; it's for anyone who dares to take Focused, Rapid, Massive Action."

INTRODUCTION

BREAKING FREE FROM THE RAT RACE: THE POWER OF THE FRMA MANTRA...

Do you ever feel like you're running endlessly but getting nowhere? Like a hamster on a wheel, you pour your time, energy, and effort into chasing success, yet your dreams remain just out of reach. Despite all your hard work, it feels like the finish line keeps moving further away.

This book isn't about running faster—it's about breaking free from that cycle altogether. It's about stepping off the wheel and charting your path. The secret lies in one powerful principle: **Focused, Rapid, Massive Action (FRMA).**

Why You Need This Book Now?

The clock is ticking. Every day you hesitate, and opportunities slip through your fingers. Yet here's the truth most people don't realize: the only thing standing between you and extraordinary success is the courage to act.

Over the past two decades, I've worked with hundreds of entrepreneurs, professionals, and business leaders—people with incredible potential who felt stuck in their careers, businesses, or lives. Some of them transformed their trajectories and achieved remarkable success. Others, unfortunately, stayed stuck. The difference? It wasn't talent, intelligence, or luck. It was **action**—the bold, focused, and decisive kind that doesn't wait for perfect conditions.

This book isn't about waiting for the stars to align. It's about creating your own constellation.

The FRMA Mantra: Your Blueprint for Success

We've all met people who seem endlessly busy but never achieve their goals. They have ideas, plans, and dreams—but something holds them back. They overthink, hesitate, or wait for the "perfect moment." That moment never comes.

Then some achieve extraordinary things, seemingly against all odds. What sets them apart? They act with focus, move with speed, and take bold, massive steps to turn their visions into reality. This is the essence of the **FRMA mantra.**

The FRMA mantra—**Focused, Rapid, Massive Action**—is not just a concept. It's a proven, practical approach to turning dreams into results. It's the force behind the real-life success stories you'll read in this book, and it's the roadmap you can follow to achieve your extraordinary results.

Meet the 10 Big Achievers

This book isn't built on theory. It's grounded in the real-life stories of **10 extraordinary achievers** (and many others) who applied the FRMA mantra to overcome obstacles, transform their lives, and achieve remarkable success. They didn't wait for perfect conditions. They faced failures, setbacks, and challenges—just like you. But they acted with purpose, speed, and boldness.

Here's a glimpse of the **10 big achievers** you'll meet in this book:

- **Alok Bector,** who built and transformed his pharmaceutical equipment business by relentlessly focusing on innovation and customer needs, even in the face of fierce competition.

- **Bhavik Vasa,** who left behind a promising career in Silicon Valley to pioneer fintech in India, acting swiftly and decisively to capitalize on a rapidly growing market.

- **Deepika Narayan Bhardwaj**, who turned personal tragedy into a national movement for justice, fearlessly challenging the legal system and creating a voice for those who had none.

- **Uday Sanghavi**, broke into tightly controlled industries by identifying key market gaps and acting boldly to disrupt the status quo.

- **Nilesh Karandikar**, built a thriving industrial manufacturing business by staying laser-focused on a specific niche, resisting distractions, and persevering through setbacks.

- **Sandeep Mall**, transformed both his business and his health by taking massive action—overhauling his lifestyle, health habits, and business strategies.

- **Gaurav Jain** acted rapidly to leave the corporate world and set up his business within months, building a successful, profitable company in his first year by seizing opportunities when others hesitated.

- **Pawan Pamecha** built a transnational business from scratch and scaled it by acting decisively in uncertain times, embracing global opportunities, and moving quickly to enter new markets.

- **Madhusudanan R** took on the challenges of the fintech space and built the most admired pioneering company by embracing bold decisions and expanding into new territories.

- **Nikhil Desai** overcame early career setbacks by embracing focused, rapid action to pivot his career and become a globally successful corporate trainer.

Each of these achievers started where you are—facing uncertainty, doubt, and fear. But they didn't let those obstacles hold them back. They moved with focus, speed, and boldness—and because of that, they became unstoppable.

✦✦✦

What You Will Learn in This Book

The FRMA mantra isn't just a mindset—it's a practical, actionable framework. By reading this book, you'll learn how to:

- **Focus** on what truly matters and eliminate distractions that drain your energy.

- **Act quickly** to build momentum, even when you don't have all the answers.

- **Take bold, massive steps** to propel yourself forward, regardless of the risks.

This book provides you with the tools, stories, and exercises to take immediate, meaningful action. Whether you're an entrepreneur, a professional, a student, or someone looking to make a major life change, FRMA will guide you from where you are now to where you want to be.

The Time to Act is Now

So, what's holding you back? If you've picked up this book, you likely have a dream—a vision of something bigger than your current reality. But maybe you've been waiting for the "right time" or the "perfect opportunity." Let me tell you this: **the perfect moment never comes.** The achievers in this book didn't wait for ideal conditions. They acted with focus, speed, and boldness. And they created their own opportunities.

Now, it's your turn. With the FRMA mantra, you have the roadmap. The stories are real. The tools are here. The only thing left is for you to take the first step.

A Personal Invitation

This isn't just a book—it's your **action plan** for a transformed life. Take notes, pause for reflection, and complete the exercises. Don't just read it—use it. This is your chance to step off the hamster wheel, take control of your destiny, and achieve what you've always known you're capable of.

Welcome to the FRMA mantra.

Welcome to your blueprint for the extraordinary.

Let's move to **Chapter 1: The Struggle of Unfulfilled Dreams**, which is designed to resonate with readers' frustrations and challenges while introducing the need for the FRMA mantra. This chapter will leverage your insights from mentoring professionals and entrepreneurs, showing the gap between effort and results, and how the real-life achievers in the book started from similar places of frustration.

THE STRUGGLE OF UNFULFILLED DREAMS

Introduction: Breaking the Cycle of Frustration

Do you feel like you're putting in endless effort but getting nowhere? Like a hamster on a wheel —running tirelessly yet stuck in the same place? You pour your energy into your dreams: working long hours, following advice, reading all the books—yet the results never seem to match your sacrifices.

Why does this happen? Why do some people effortlessly achieve their biggest goals while others, despite their relentless hard work, remain stuck?

This struggle is more common than you think. The problem isn't that you are not working hard enough; it's that you're missing a critical factor: *Focused, Rapid, Massive Action (FRMA).*

Why Hard Work Alone Isn't Enough

We have been told for years that success is about hard work, perseverance, and luck. But if that were true, wouldn't everyone who works hard be wildly successful?

Here's the truth: Success doesn't come from hard work alone. It comes from a specific kind of action—a relentless, intentional, and fearless approach that separates dreamers from doers.

Why do so many people remain stuck?

1. They overthink every step, waiting for the "perfect" moment.

2. They fear failure and allow it to paralyze them.

3. They chase too many goals, spreading themselves too thin and losing clarity.

Sounds familiar? If so, it's time to stop spinning your wheels. It's time to adopt a sharper, bolder, and more powerful approach: *Focused, Rapid, Massive Action (FRMA)*.

The FRMA Mantra

FRMA—Focused, Rapid, Massive Action—is the answer. It's not about wishful thinking, half-hearted attempts, or waiting for the stars to align. It's about **acting with clarity, speed, and boldness** to make meaningful progress toward your goals.

- **Focused Action**: Identify your single most important goal and commit to it fully.

- **Rapid Action**: Move quickly, seizing opportunities before they slip away.

- **Massive Action**: Think big, act with intensity, and go all in—because half-measures lead to half-results.

FRMA is more than just a strategy; it's a mindset. And it's the mindset that transformed the lives of people who were once in the same place as you—stuck, frustrated, and seeking more.

Real-Life Stories of Transformation

This isn't a theory. The FRMA mantra has led to real-life transformations for countless individuals who dared to act.

Let's look at three achievers who broke free from the cycle of frustration and turned their lives around.

1. Alok Bector: Redefining the Competitive Edge

When Alok entered the pharmaceutical equipment industry, he faced well-established giants. His small business struggled under the shadow of these competitors. Yet, instead of being overwhelmed, Alok chose to focus on one thing: **Innovation.**

He poured every resource and ounce of energy into making his product the best in the market. His relentless commitment to innovation, combined with rapid and massive action, enabled him to outpace competitors and achieve remarkable success.

FRMA Insight: Alok succeeded not by doing everything, but by channelling his energy with unmatched intensity toward a single, transformative goal.

2. Nikhil Desai: Moving Fast in a Crisis

When the pandemic hit, Nikhil's career as a corporate trainer came to a halt. While many of his peers waited for conditions to "return to normal" Nikhil chose a different path. He adapted—quickly. He transitioned his training programs online, he built a global audience within months.

What could have been a setback became his biggest breakthrough.

FRMA Insight: Nikhil's willingness to act rapidly, even in uncertain times, and unlocked opportunities that would have remained closed had he waited.

3. Sandeep Mall: Choosing Bold, Massive Action

As a business owner, Sandeep faced challenges in both his personal and professional life. His health was deteriorating, and his business had stagnated. Instead of making small, cautious changes, he opted for massive action.

He overhauled his lifestyle, adopted a rigorous fitness regime, and revamped his business strategies. His bold decisions not only revitalized his health but also reignited his business.

FRMA Insight: Sandeep's story demonstrates that sometimes small steps are not enough. True transformation demands bold, massive action.

What's Holding You Back?

If you see yourself in these stories, you're not alone. The barriers to success are universal, but they can be overcome with the FRMA mindset.

Here are the three most common barriers that keep people stuck:

1. **Scattered Focus**: Trying to do everything at once dilutes your energy and hinders meaningful progress.

2. **Fear of Failure**: The "what if it goes wrong" mindset is paralyzing, preventing you from taking bold steps necessary for growth.

3. **Waiting for the Right Time**: Perfectionism leads to procrastination. The perfect time doesn't exist—there's only now.

Reflective Pause

Take a moment to reflect:

- What's the one area in your life where you're holding back?

- Where are you hesitating—fearing failure or waiting for ideal conditions?

- What's one bold action you could take today if you embraced the FRMA mindset?

Key Takeaways

- Success isn't just about hard work; it's about **Focused, Rapid, Massive Action.**

- Real achievers don't wait for the perfect time—they create their opportunities by acting now.

- You don't need more resources, connections, or luck. What you need is the will to act with clarity, speed, and boldness.

A Preview of What's Next

Ready to break free from the endless cycle and step into a more focused, purposeful way of achieving success? In the next chapter, we'll uncover the secrets of the **Focus** component of the FRMA mantra. Discover practical tools to silence distractions, pinpoint what truly matters, and unlock a laser-sharp clarity that transforms your efforts into tangible results. Get ready to take control and start seeing the breakthroughs you've been waiting for!

FRMA MANTRA – YOUR BLUEPRINT FOR EXTRAORDINARY SUCCESS

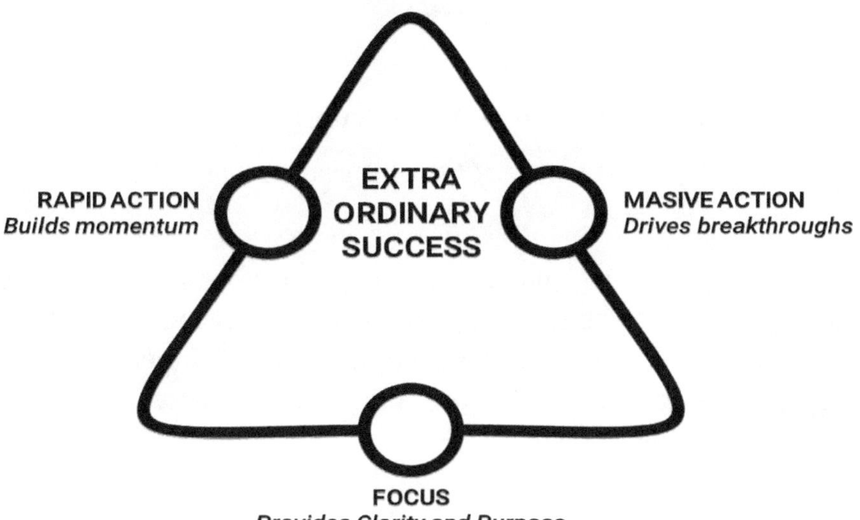

Introduction: The Power of the FRMA Mantra

Welcome to the core of this book: the **FRMA mantra.** This isn't just another motivational phrase—it's a paradigm shift. It's a proven, actionable framework that has empowered ordinary people to achieve extraordinary success.

If you've ever felt that traditional advice like "work hard" or "be patient" isn't enough, you're not alone. And you are right—hard work alone won't get you to the finish line. What you need is the **right kind of action**—taken at the **right time**, with the **right intensity**.

This is the essence of **Focused, Rapid, Massive Action (FRMA)**: a mindset and strategy designed to transform effort into exponential results.

◆◆◆

Breaking Down the FRMA Mantra

FRMA is built on three interconnected principles—**Focus, Rapid Action**, and **Massive Action.** These elements function like the gears of a well-oiled machine, driving you steadily toward extraordinary success.

Let's explore each component in detail.

✦✦✦

1. Focused Action: Zero in on What Truly Matters

"Focus is the art of knowing what to ignore."

— James Clear

Focus isn't about doing more—it's about doing less—but with laser-sharp precision. It's about eliminating distractions and channelling your energy to actions that align directly with your highest goals.

Most people don't fail because they lack effort; they fail because their efforts are scattered. Juggling too many priorities dilutes their focus and, ultimately, their results.

Focused Actions	Distractions
Prioritizing one key goal	Multitasking on low-impact tasks
Setting a clear deadline	Waiting for inspiration to strike
Saying "no" to irrelevant tasks	Trying to do everything at once
Tracking measurable progress	Worrying about others' opinions

Case Study: Nilesh Karandikar's Journey to Market Domination

Nilesh, an industrial manufacturing entrepreneur, was drowning in distractions and struggling to gain traction. He made the bold decision to specialize in a niche market—industrial manipulators for assembly lines. By focusing exclusively on this area, he became the go-to expert and left his competitors far behind.

FRMA Insight: Nilesh's story shows that focus isn't just about prioritizing—it's about saying "no" to everything that doesn't serve your core goal.

Key Lesson: Focus creates clarity and channels your energy where it matters most, amplifying your progress exponentially.

Take Action Now: Your Focus Blueprint What's the one goal that will make the biggest impact on your life? Use the template below to define your focus and eliminate distractions:

Interactive Template: FRMA Personal Blueprint *(Include the template table here, as suggested above.)*

Component	Your Goal or Action
Focus	What is your ONE most important goal?
Rapid Action	What opportunity can you act on immediately?
Massive Action	What bold move can you take to accelerate results?

Distraction Audit Before you can focus, you need to identify what's pulling you away. Fill in the following table to perform your distraction audit:

Distraction	Impact on Goal	Plan to Eliminate
Example: Social Media	Wastes 2 hours daily	Schedule 30 min blocks
Example: Low-priority tasks	Dilutes focus	Delegate or say "no"

2. Rapid Action: Speed is Your Secret Weapon

"To get ahead, you must act quickly and decisively. Speed creates momentum."

One of the greatest obstacles to success is hesitation. Many people wait for the "perfect" moment to act, but here's the truth: **perfection is the enemy of progress.** If you wait for ideal conditions, you'll be waiting forever.

Rapid Action is about seizing opportunities in the moment. Acting quickly creates momentum, and momentum is the driving force behind success.

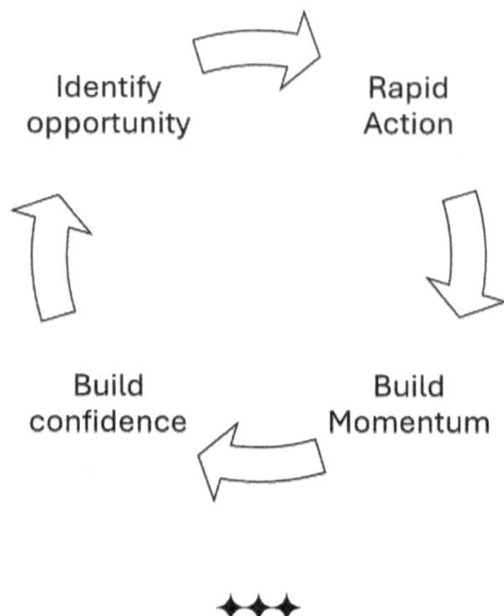

◆◆◆

Story of Gaurav Jain – Launching a Business in Record Time

After years of climbing the corporate ladder, Gaurav Jain decided to take the leap into entrepreneurship. Instead of waiting for the perfect business plan or ideal timing, he launched his company within months of leaving his job. In his first year, he secured 15 clients, outpacing competitors who were still planning their next move.

FRMA Insight: Gaurav's rapid action allowed him to gain early momentum and capitalize on opportunities others missed.

Key Lesson: Speed is often the difference between seizing an opportunity and watching it slip away.

Rapid Action Exercise: Build Your Momentum:

Momentum starts with small, fast steps. Identify an opportunity and take immediate action using the template below:

Interactive Template: Rapid Action Tracker

A simple table for you to log your quick actions and track momentum.

Opportunity	Action Taken	Time to Execute	Outcome
Launch business idea	Created a pitch deck	2 days	Scheduled first meeting
Respond to client lead	Sent proposal email	30 minutes	Secured a follow-up call

3. Massive Action: Playing Small Won't Get You Big Results

"Massive action is what separates dreamers from doers. Playing small gets small results."

Massive Action isn't about playing it safe—it is about stepping out of your comfort zone, setting audacious goals, and committing fully to achieving them. While small actions may maintain the status quo, massive action has the power to spark real breakthroughs.

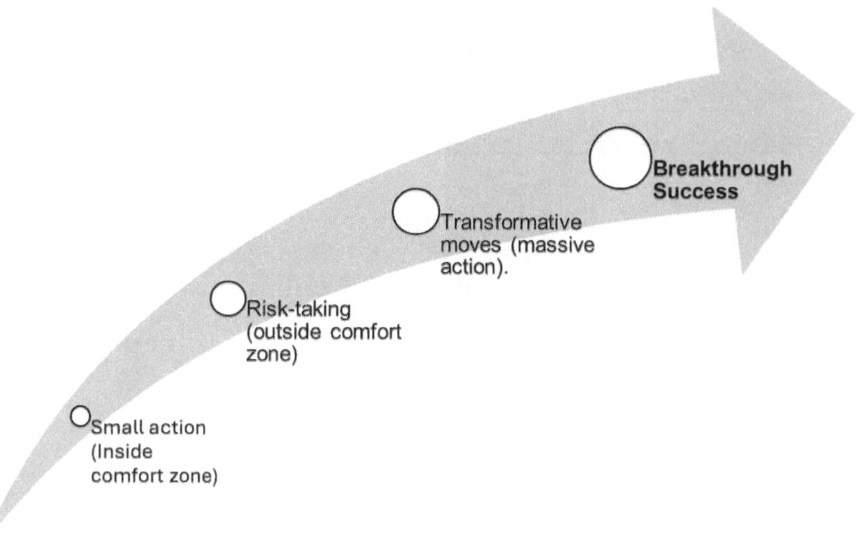

Story of Sandeep Mall's Transformative Decision

Sandeep Mall, a business owner, found himself at a crossroads, grappling with stagnation in his personal and professional life.

Instead of making incremental changes, he made a bold decision: he committed to massive action.

He transformed his lifestyle, adopting a rigorous fitness regime that redefined his health and energy levels. Simultaneously he restructured his business strategies, bringing fresh perspective and dynamic changes to his operation. The result? A revitalized health profile and a business that went from struggling to thriving.

FRMA Insight: Sandeep's journey shows that extraordinary results demand extraordinary commitments.

Key Lesson:

Massive action propels you beyond your limits, unlocking opportunities and achievements you never imagined.

Massive Action Challenge: Commit to Bold Moves

Breakthroughs aren't born from hesitation—they come from bold, decisive actions.

Use the Massive Action Ladder to assess where you stand and the Commitment Sheet to declare your next bold step:

Interactive Template: Massive Action Ladder *(Include the ladder graphic here.)*

Interactive Template: Massive Action Commitment Sheet

A motivational contract readers fill out to commit to bold, transformative steps.

Template Example:

I, [Name], commit to taking the following massive action by [Deadline]:

Action: [Describe bold move].

Expected Impact: [How this will advance my goal].

Signed: [Signature].

✦✦✦

Why FRMA Works

Each component of FRMA—Focus, Rapid Action, and Massive Action—is powerful on its own. But when combined, they create a multiplier effect that drives exponential success.

Here's how it works:

1. **Focus** eliminates distractions, giving you clarity on what truly matters.

2. **Rapid Action** builds momentum, turning ideas into opportunities.

3. **Massive Action** drives breakthroughs and accelerates growth.

When you adopt the FRMA mindset, you move beyond working hard—you start working smart, fast, and boldly. This is a game-changing formula that transforms dreamers into achievers.

Key Takeaways for Chapter 2

- **Focus** means narrowing your attention to what truly matters and saying no to distractions.

- **Rapid Action** means making quick, decisive moves to build momentum.

- **Massive Action** means stepping out of your comfort zone to take bold, transformative steps.

- When combined, Focused, Rapid, and Massive Action leads to extraordinary results.

- Real-life achievers like Nilesh Karandikar, Gaurav Jain, and Sandeep Mall have used FRMA to overcome obstacles and achieve remarkable success.

Your FRMA Toolkit

Now that you've explored Focus, Rapid Action, and Massive Action, it's time to put everything together. Use the templates below to start building your own FRMA plan:

- **Focus Blueprint**: Define your primary goal and eliminate distractions.

- **Rapid Action Tracker**: Log quick actions to build momentum and create consistent progress.

- **Massive Action Commitment Sheet**: Declare your boldest steps and commit to actions that lead to transformative breakthroughs.

1. FRMA Personal Blueprint Template

A worksheet readers can fill in to align their goals with the FRMA principles.

Component	Your Goal or Action
Focus	What is your ONE most important goal?
Rapid Action	What opportunity can you act on immediately?
Massive Action	What bold move can you take to accelerate results?

2. Distraction Audit

A tool to help readers identify and eliminate distractions.

Distraction	Impact on Goal	Plan to Eliminate
Example: Social Media	Wastes 2 hours daily	Schedule 30 min blocks
Example: Low-priority tasks	Dilutes focus	Delegate or say "no"

3. Rapid Action Tracker

A simple table for readers to log their quick actions and track momentum.

Opportunity	Action Taken	Time to Execute	Outcome
Launch business idea	Created a pitch deck	2 days	Scheduled first meeting
Respond to client lead	Sent proposal email	30 minutes	Secured a follow-up call

What's Next?

Your transformation starts here.In the next chapter, we'll take a deep dive into the first component of FRMA: **Focus.** You'll discover how to eliminate distractions, sharpen your vision, and channel your energy into actions that truly matter. Get ready to unlock the power of focused action and set the foundation for exponential success.

GETTING FOCUSED – SHARPENING YOUR VISION

"The successful warrior is the average man, with laser-like focus."

– Bruce Lee

In today's world, distractions are everywhere. We're bombarded from every angle, from endless notifications to a constant influx of new information. The temptation to chase every opportunity, respond to every email, and take every call is real, but here's the truth: trying to do everything is the fastest way to achieve nothing.

True success isn't about doing more—it's about doing less with unwavering, purposeful focus. The most successful people don't chase every opportunity. Instead, they identify the one or two crucial areas that truly matter and dedicate their energy to mastering them.

In this chapter, we'll explore the first pillar of the FRMA mantra: **Focus**. You'll discover how some of the most successful people I've mentored achieved extraordinary results. By cutting through the noise, zeroing in on what truly moves the needle, and refusing to be distracted by anything less. Now, it's your turn.

Why Focus is the Foundation of Success

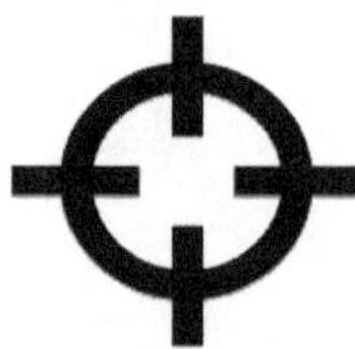

Think about your typical day. How often do you find yourself bouncing between tasks—emails, meetings, notifications—only to end the day feeling like you've accomplished nothing substantial? This is the curse of being scattered. Without focus, even the most talented and hardworking people can struggle to make meaningful progress.

The focus is clarity. It's about knowing exactly what you want and dedicating all your energy, time, and resources toward that one goal. Without focus, you're just spinning your wheels, expending energy on things that won't drive you forward.

*"You will never reach your destination if you stop
and throw stones at every dog that barks."*

– Winston Churchill

The achievers featured in this book understood that focus is more than a strategy; it's a mindset. They recognized that to accomplish something significant, they had to eliminate distractions and narrow their efforts to the most impactful actions.

Story: Nilesh Karandikar – The Power of Niche Focus

When Nilesh Karandikar launched his industrial manufacturing business, he faced a challenge familiar to many entrepreneurs: the urge to do everything. Initially, he believed that by offering a wide variety of products and serving multiple markets, he would accelerate his growth. But after years of slow progress, Nilesh discovered a powerful truth: **trying to be everything to everyone was holding him back.**

Nilesh made a bold decision to focus exclusively on a single niche—developing industrial manipulators for specific assembly lines. It wasn't an obvious or glamorous choice, but by dedicating all his energy to mastering this one area, he transformed his business. His reputation for expertise grew, and soon his company became a leader in this specialized field.

Nilesh's journey teaches us a critical lesson: Focus breeds clarity, and clarity builds unmatched expertise—the kind of expertise that leads to breakthrough success.

How to Develop Laser-Sharp Focus

1. Define Your Core Goal

Ask yourself: **What is the one goal that, if achieved, would create the biggest positive impact on your life or business?** This is your North Star—the guiding light that directs your focus and efforts.

Write it down, and be as specific as possible. Clarity is key to turning aspirations into actionable steps.

"Success demands singleness of purpose."

– Vince Lombardi

2. Eliminate the Non-Essentials

Your time and energy are your most valuable resources—and they're finite. Every task you take on that doesn't align with your core goal drains resources from what truly matters. Take a moment to list out the activities, commitments, and distractions that don't contribute to your primary objective. Then, make the tough but necessary choices: eliminate, delegate, or defer these non-essential tasks.

3. Create Routines and Boundaries

Designate specific blocks of time for focused work and protect them fiercely. During these periods, resist the urge to check emails, or respond to notifications. Establishing clear routines and boundaries sends a powerful message to yourself and others: this time is sacred for working on what matters.

4. Set Micro-Goals to Track Progress

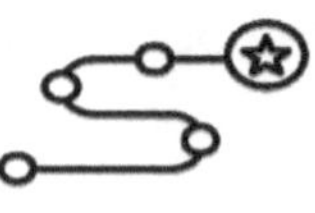

Break your primary goal into smaller, achievable milestones. These micro-goals serve as checkpoints, keeping you on course and building momentum as you achieve each one.

◆◆◆

Actionable Takeaway

Take a few minutes right now to define your core goal.

Ask yourself: ***What is the single most important goal that I need to achieve to make the biggest impact in my life or business?*** Write it down and commit to focusing all your energy and resources toward it.

Then, list out three distractions or non-essential activities that you can eliminate or reduce to free up time for this goal. Implement this immediately.

Key Takeaways:

- **Focus** is the art of elimination—it's knowing what to ignore so that you can devote all your energy to what truly matters.

- **Eliminate distractions** and cut down on non-essential tasks. Focus doesn't mean working harder; it means working smarter.

- **Set clear goals and boundaries** that protect your time and energy for the tasks that drive the greatest results.

With your focus sharpened, you're now ready to turn clarity into meaningful progress. In the next chapter, we'll dive into the next pillar of the FRMA mantra—**Rapid Action.** You'll learn why acting swiftly on opportunities is critical and how you can make speed a habit in your journey to success.

 With your focus sharpened and your distractions cleared away, you're now ready to take the next step in transforming your goals into reality. But focus alone isn't enough. Success favours those who act quickly, and who don't hesitate when opportunities arise.

In the next chapter, we'll explore the power of Rapid Action—how to harness the energy you've built through focus and turn it into swift, decisive moves that propel you forward. Get ready to make speed your ally and seize opportunities before they pass you by.

SPEED MATTERS – THE POWER OF RAPID ACTION

"The greatest danger in life is not taking action in time."

— **Confucius**

In both life and business, speed is often the most underrated advantages. Many believe that success comes from meticulous planning and waiting for the perfect moment. **But while they wait, opportunities slip away.** Success favours those who move quickly, make decisive choices, and seize opportunities before they disappear.

Before diving deeper into the power of **Rapid Action**, it is important to understand a critical distinction: **acting rapidly versus merely acting fast.**

Rapid action isn't about rushing or acting impulsively. It's about moving with intention—taking focused, purposeful steps in the right direction. In contrast, fast action without a clear plan leads to mistakes, wasted energy, and missed opportunities.

Remember: Rapid action is deliberate and calculated. It creates momentum, builds confidence, and leads to tangible results. Moving quickly without direction might feel productive, but it can easily veer off course.

Why Speed is Your Secret Weapon

"Move fast, and break things."

— **Mark Zuckerberg**

In today's fast-paced world, speed is a key competitive advantage. The faster you act, the quicker you can learn, adapt, and improve. While others are held back by indecision, you're gaining real-world experience. **Speed isn't about recklessness—it's about making informed decisions and taking immediate action.**

Waiting for perfect conditions is a common trap .The truth is, perfection is rarely attainable, and the pursuit of it often leads to stagnation. Instead, speed generates momentum, and that momentum becomes the driving force behind lasting success.

"The way to get started is to quit talking and begin doing."

– **Walt Disney**

✦✦✦

Story of Gaurav Jain – Launching a Successful Business in Record Time

When Gaurav Jain left his corporate job to start his own business, he didn't waste any time. Within a few months, he had launched his company and secured his first 15 clients. His success wasn't the result of a flawless plan—it stemmed from his ability to act quickly, make decisions fast, and seize opportunities as they arose.

Gaurav didn't wait for ideal conditions or spend months perfecting his business plan. Instead, he took action immediately, leveraged his network, and secured clients before his business was fully established. By the time others might have been preparing to start, Gaurav was already ahead of the curve.

The Lesson: Success often rewards those who act fast and decisively. Gaurav's journey highlights how speed not only builds momentum but also unlocks opportunities that lead to accelerated growth.

✦✦✦

Overcoming the Fear of Acting Quickly

One of the biggest reasons people hesitate to act quickly is fear: fear of making the wrong decision, fear of failure, fear of moving too fast. Here's the truth: **speed is more valuable than perfection.** Successful people recognize that mistakes are part of the process—they learn from each experience and adjust as they go.

"Indecision is the thief of opportunity."

– Jim Rohn

The real danger lies not in moving too quickly but in moving too slowly. Taking too long to decide often means someone else will seize the opportunity you hesitated over. The cost of inaction far outweighs the cost of a mistake.

How to Develop the Habit of Rapid Action

Speed is a skill you can cultivate. It's not about acting recklessly; it's about making informed decisions swiftly. Here's how to start:

1. **Set Decision Deadlines**

   Set a deadline for every major decision—whether it's a business strategy, career choice, or new opportunity. Avoid the trap of overthinking. Instead, commit to making the decision within your timeline and immediately take the next step.

2. **Start Small, Move Fast**

   Begin with smaller, quicker decisions to build confidence and comfort with speed. Over time, you'll be able to make larger decisions swiftly. Give yourself a deadline for every major decision—whether it's a business strategy, career choice, or opportunity. Resist overthinking; make the decision and take the next step.

3. Don't Wait for Perfect Conditions

Perfect conditions rarely exist. When you see an opportunity, seize it. Act now and adjust along the way.

"Do not wait: the time will never be 'just right.' Start where you stand, and work with whatever tools you may have at your command."

– Napoleon Hill

The Power of Momentum

When you act quickly, you create **momentum**. This momentum fosters a sense of accomplishment, which in turn boosts confidence and fuels further action. When you delay, you lose energy, confidence, and opportunities.

The faster you act, the more opportunities you generate. Even if some actions lead to failures, they're part of the journey toward success. Small wins eventually pave the way for major victories.

Momentum is the fuel that turns dreams into reality. Keep moving forward, even if only in small steps—you'll eventually reach your goals.

Why Rapid Action Transforms Goals into Reality

Many people dream big but never take the crucial step to act on their ideas. They spend months or even years, planning and waiting for the "right moment." But success doesn't favor perpetual planners—it belongs to doers. Those who aren't afraid to act, even when the path is unclear, create opportunities and achieve their goals.

"Action is the foundational key to all success."

– Pablo Picasso

Summary: The Power of Rapid Action

- **Speed is a competitive edge** in today's fast-moving world, creating momentum and opening up opportunities that may not last.

- **Gaurav Jain's story** shows that acting quickly allows you to capture opportunities and build rapid growth.

- **Overcome the fear of fast action** by accepting mistakes as part of the process; remember, inaction is often riskier than a mistake.

- **Develop the habit of rapid action** by setting deadlines for decisions, starting with small steps, and never waiting for perfect conditions.

- **Momentum fuels success**—the more you act, the more opportunities you create.

Actionable Takeaway

Think about a decision or opportunity you've been delaying—whether it's starting a project, applying for that dream job, or pursuing a business idea. Commit to making a choice today. Set a clear deadline for your first step and take action immediately. You'll be amazed at how one decisive move can build momentum and unlock new possibilities.

Transition to the Next Chapter

Speed is crucial, but it's only part of the equation. To achieve extraordinary results, you need to combine speed with **Massive Action**.

In the next chapter, we'll explore how to take bold, transformative steps toward your goals. Get ready to embrace a level of action that will push you beyond limits and drive exponential growth.

BOLD MOVES – THE GAME-CHANGING EFFECT OF MASSIVE ACTION

"The path to success is to take massive, determined action."

– Tony Robbins

In a world where playing it safe is the norm, **massive action** is the game-changer that separates winners from the crowd. Most people tread cautiously, taking small, calculated steps, hoping these will eventually lead to big results. While incremental progress has its merits, the reality is this: **real breakthroughs occur when you make bold, transformative leaps.**

Massive action is not about recklessness; it's about courage. It's about making decisions that push you beyond your comfort zone, embracing risks others avoid, and fully committing to your goals. It's uncomfortable —absolutely—but it's also where the magic happens.

In this chapter, we'll uncover the **life-changing power of massive action** and how it can unlock extraordinary results for you in both your personal and professional life.

Why Massive Action Leads to Breakthroughs

"You are confined only by the walls you build yourself."

– Andrew Murphy

Small actions can make you feel productive—but they rarely lead to transformative change. Massive action, on the other hand, demands that you think bigger, act boldly, and break free from the status quo. It forces you to operate at a higher level, where the risks may be greater, but the rewards are far beyond anything small steps can achieve.

Massive action does more than move the needle—**it reshapes your reality**. It's the catalyst that breaks through fear, self-doubt, and inertia, propelling you into uncharted territory where true growth happens.

"Go big or go home."

– Eliza Dushku

When you take massive action, you shatter the walls of limitation and build unstoppable momentum. This isn't just about doing more; it's about doing what scares you, what feels impossible. That's where the breakthroughs live.

Story of Sandeep Mall – Transforming Health and Business Through Massive Action

Sandeep Mall's story perfectly illustrates the transformative power of massive action. At one point, Sandeep found himself in a rut—his business had hit a plateau, and his health was rapidly deteriorating. He knew that incremental changes wouldn't be enough to turn things around. What he needed was massive action.

Sandeep made a bold decision: he committed to an intense fitness regimen that completely revitalized his health in just a few months. At the same time, he restructured his business, made difficult yet necessary decisions, and ventured into untested markets. It wasn't easy, and it wasn't comfortable—but the results were extraordinary.

His health dramatically improved, giving him the energy and clarity to take his business to unprecedented heights. By embracing massive action, Sandeep didn't just make small improvements; he transformed his entire life—both personally and professionally.

The Lesson: Massive action is about going all-in. It's about making bold moves that others avoid, and when you commit fully, the results can be life-changing.

Why Playing Small Leads to Small Results

"If you want something you've never had, you must be willing to do something you've never done."

– Thomas Jefferson

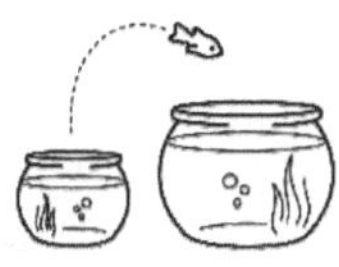

Most people avoid massive action because they fear failure, discomfort, or the unknown. Instead, they play it safe—sticking to what's familiar and predictable. But here's the hard truth: **playing small will never lead to big results.**

Incremental steps feel reassuring, but they also keep you firmly anchored within your comfort zone. Massive action, however, challenges you to step into the unknown. It's about taking calculated risks, embracing discomfort, and committing to goals that feel audacious or even impossible.

Massive action isn't easy—but it's necessary. The bigger the risk, the bigger the reward. While playing it safe may provide temporary comfort, but that same comfort becomes the enemy of growth. Bold moves, on the other hand, create the momentum and opportunities needed for breakthroughs.

How to Take Massive Action in Your Life

Massive action is about taking bold, calculated steps that push you beyond your limits. Here's how to start:

1. **Set Audacious Goals**

    Don't aim for minor improvements. Aim higher—set goals that challenge you—and make you question whether they're even achievable. These are the goals worth pursuing.

2. **Commit Fully**

    Massive action demands unwavering commitment. Half-hearted efforts won't cut it. Decide what you truly want, and then give it everything you've got—no holding back, no excuses.

3. **Push Through Fear**

    Fear is a sign you're stepping out of your comfort zone, and that's exactly where growth happens. Use fear as a guide—if it scares you, it's probably worth doing.

4. **Take Immediate Action**

    Don't wait. The longer you delay, the harder it becomes to take bold steps. Once you've identified your goal, act immediately—even if it feels uncomfortable.

"Take massive action. The results will follow."

– **Tony Robbins**

Why Boldness Creates Opportunities

Massive action creates **opportunities that would** otherwise remain out of reach. When you take bold steps, you distinguish yourself from the crowd. People notice your commitment and take you seriously. Doors that once seemed closed begin to open because boldness attracts attention and earns respect.

Taking massive action inspires others and creates a ripple effect. **The world rewards boldness.** Whether it's financial success, personal growth, or new relationships, the rewards of boldness far outweigh the risks.

Summary: The Power of Massive Action

- **Massive action creates breakthroughs.** Small steps lead to small results, but bold moves lead to transformative growth.

- **Sandeep Mall's** story demonstrates how committing to massive action can lead to dramatic improvements in both health and business.

- **Playing small leads to predictable, incremental progress.** To achieve extraordinary results, you must take extraordinary risks.

- **Start taking massive action** by setting audacious goals, committing fully, pushing through fear, and acting immediately.

- **Boldness creates opportunities.** When you act boldly, you inspire others and open doors that playing small never could.

Actionable Takeaway

Think about one bold, massive action you've been putting off—whether it's launching a business, making a career pivot, or pursuing a life-changing goal. Now write it down. This is your moment to commit. The first step is all it takes. Yes, it might feel uncomfortable or scary, but that's where growth happens. Take that step today. Massive action doesn't wait. It starts now.

✦✦✦

Next Chapter: The Big Achievers Who Made It Happen

 Now that you understand the transformative power of massive action, it's time to meet the real-life achievers who've applied the FRMA mantra to achieve extraordinary success. In the next chapter, you'll dive into their stories, drawing inspiration and insights from their journeys of Focused, Rapid, Massive Action.

✦✦✦

THE BIG ACHIEVERS WHO MADE IT HAPPEN

"Success leaves clues, and if you follow the actions of successful people, you can create success for yourself."

– Tony Robbins

By now, you've learned about the power of **Focused, Rapid, Massive Action (FRMA)** and how it can propel you toward extraordinary achievements. But FRMA isn't just an abstract concept—it's a strategy proven in real life. This chapter brings you stories of 10 exceptional achievers who faced challenges, took bold steps, and applied FRMA to turn their dreams into reality.

These stories are more than just inspiring anecdotes; they are a **roadmap for action.** Each achiever showcases a unique element of FRMA—whether it's laser-sharp focus, rapid decision-making, or transformative massive action. As you read their journeys, you'll find practical lessons and strategies you can adopt to create your own breakthroughs.

1. Alok Bector: Mastering Innovation Through Focused Action

Entering the fiercely competitive world of pharmaceutical equipment, Alok Bector faced giants with more resources and market share. Instead of trying to compete on all fronts, Alok chose to focus on one: **innovation**.

He directed all his energy toward making his products better, faster, and more efficient than anything else on the market. This relentless focus on innovation not only differentiated his company but also won contracts with some of the industry's biggest players.

Key FRMA Lesson: Focus

Alok's success came from his unwavering focus on innovation. His story proves that focus is the foundation of mastery and allows you to dominate your niche.

2. Bhavik Vasa: Seizing Opportunities with Rapid Action

Leaving a lucrative career in Silicon Valley, Bhavik Vasa saw an emerging opportunity in India's fintech space. He didn't wait for perfect conditions—he acted swiftly, launching a fintech platform and forming strategic partnerships within months.

By moving quickly, Bhavik gained a first-mover advantage and positioned his company as an industry leader before competitors even entered the space.

Key FRMA Lesson: Rapid Action

Bhavik's story highlights the power of acting fast. When you seize opportunities with speed, you create momentum that others can't catch up to.

3. Deepika Narayan Bhardwaj: Fearless Advocacy Through Massive Action

A personal tragedy could have silenced Deepika Narayan Bhardwaj, but instead, she turned her pain into purpose. She became a fearless advocate for justice, creating documentaries that exposed systemic legal injustices. Her bold actions sparked a nationwide movement for reform.

Key FRMA Lesson: Massive Action

Deepika's journey shows the transformative power of massive action. She didn't take small, cautious steps—she went all in, creating bold, lasting change in society.

4. Uday Sanghavi: Disrupting the Market Through Focus

By focusing exclusively on custom automation solutions in the packaging machinery sector, Uday Sanghavi disrupted an industry dominated by major players. His specialized, innovative products carved out a niche that made him a market leader.

Key FRMA Lesson: Focus

Uday's story underscores the importance of concentrating your efforts on a specific niche. His ability to focus created differentiation and long-term success.

5. Nilesh Karandikar: Building a Niche Empire with Laser Focus

Rather than spreading his business thin, Nilesh Karandikar zeroed in on a single niche: industrial manipulators for assembly lines. By becoming an expert in this field, Nilesh built a thriving empire that competitors struggled to match.

Key FRMA Lesson: Focus

Nilesh's journey is a testament to the power of specialization. Focus creates expertise, reputation, and sustainable growth.

6. Sandeep Mall: Personal and Business Transformation Through Massive Action

Facing a stagnant business and declining health, Sandeep Mall knew small changes wouldn't suffice. He overhauled his life with an intense fitness regimen and bold business decisions. His transformative actions revitalized both his health and his company, leading to extraordinary outcomes.

Key FRMA Lesson: Massive Action

Sandeep's story illustrates that massive action creates massive transformation. Small steps can't achieve the dramatic breakthroughs bold moves can.

✦✦✦

7. Gaurav Jain: Speed as a Competitive Edge

When Gaurav Jain transitioned from corporate life to entrepreneurship, he understood that speed was his greatest ally. Within months, he launched his business and secured multiple clients, leaving competitors in his wake.

Key FRMA Lesson: Rapid Action

Gaurav's journey demonstrates that speed not only builds momentum but also establishes an early advantage in competitive markets.

✦✦✦

8. Pawan Pamecha: Scaling Globally Through Massive Action

Pawan Pamecha didn't hesitate when an opportunity to expand internationally presented itself. He embraced the challenge and took bold steps to scale his business globally, transforming it into a global powerhouse.

Key FRMA Lesson: Massive Action

Pawan's story shows that exponential growth demands bold, fearless decisions. Playing small simply doesn't lead to global success.

✦✦✦

9. Madhusudanan R: Embracing Challenges with Rapid Action

Recognizing the fintech industry's untapped potential, Madhusudanan R launched his platform without waiting for ideal conditions. His quick, decisive actions secured partnerships and positioned him as a pioneer in a growing market.

Key FRMA Lesson: Rapid Action

Madhusudanan's journey highlights that speed is often the critical edge that separates leaders from followers.

10. Nikhil Desai: Turning Setbacks Into Success Through Focus and Rapid Action

Despite facing early career setbacks, Nikhil Desai used them as fuel to focus on his personal growth and act quickly when opportunities arose. His resilience and rapid actions led him to become a globally renowned corporate trainer.

Key FRMA Lesson: Focus and Rapid Action

Nikhil's story reminds us that setbacks are just stepping stones. With focus and decisive action, they can lead to incredible success.

Summary: Lessons from the FRMA Achievers

The journeys of these 10 achievers highlight the immense power of **Focused, Rapid, Massive Action:**

- **Focus** helps you master your niche, as seen in the stories of Alok Bector, Uday Sanghavi, and Nilesh Karandikar.

- **Rapid Action** creates momentum and opportunities, as demonstrated by Bhavik Vasa, Gaurav Jain, and Madhusudanan R.

- **Massive Action** drives transformation and exponential growth, as exemplified by Deepika Narayan Bhardwaj, Sandeep Mall, and Pawan Pamecha.

These achievers didn't wait for perfect conditions. They acted with purpose, speed, and boldness—proving that **success isn't accidental—it's intentional.**

Actionable Takeaway

Choose one of these achievers' stories that resonates most with you. Is it Alok Bector's relentless focus on innovation, Bhavik Vasa's fearless rapid action, or another bold leap that speaks to your journey?

Identify the FRMA principle that played the biggest role in their success—whether it's focus, rapid action, or massive action.

Apply that principle to your life today. Take one bold step toward your biggest goal and commit fully.

Because here's the truth: Success doesn't wait. Neither should you.

Transition to the Next Chapter

 Now that you've seen the power of FRMA in action, it's time to address the challenges that might hold you back. In the next chapter, "Overcoming Common Obstacles to FRMA," we'll tackle the fears, doubts, and roadblocks that stop most people from embracing Focused, Rapid, Massive Action—and how to overcome them.

OVERCOMING COMMON OBSTACLES TO FRMA

"Doubt kills more dreams than failure ever will."

– **Suzy Kassem**

You've witnessed the extraordinary power of **Focused, Rapid, Massive Action (FRMA)** in the stories of big achievers. But let's face it—life isn't without challenges. Fear, doubt, and setbacks lurk at every corner. The truth is, **success isn't about avoiding obstacles; it's about learning how to overcome them.**

In this chapter, we'll explore the most common challenges people encounter when applying the FRMA mantra and provide actionable strategies to overcome them. The path to success is not linear, but with the right mindset and tools, you can conquer anything that stands in your way.

1. The Fear of Failure

"The only thing we have to fear is fear itself."

– **Franklin D. Roosevelt**

Fear of failure is a paralyzing force. It holds people back from taking risks, chasing dreams, and acting boldly. Yet, every great achiever understands one key truth: **failure is a stepping stone to success, not the end of the road.**

Story: Deepika Narayan Bhardwaj – Facing Fear with Boldness

Deepika faced the daunting challenge of standing up for an unpopular cause. The fear of societal judgment and failure loomed large, but she chose boldness over hesitation. By confronting her fears, she became a fearless advocate for justice, transforming countless lives and sparking systemic change.

How to Overcome the Fear of Failure:

- **Reframe Failure as Feedback**: View every failure as a learning opportunity. Ask, "What can I learn from this?" rather than "Why did I fail?"

- **Take Small Steps**: Build confidence by starting with manageable risks. Each success, no matter how small, reduces fear.

- **Visualize the Worst-Case Scenario**: Imagine the worst that could happen. Once you confront and accept it , fear loses its grip.

2. Overthinking and Analysis Paralysis

"Indecision is often worse than wrong action."

– Jerry Brown

Overthinking is the silent killer of progress. It traps people in endless loops of planning and analysis, robbing them of momentum. **Perfection is a myth—progress comes from acting, learning, and refining along the way.**

Story: Bhavik Vasa – Moving Fast and Adjusting on the Go

Bhavik didn't wait for perfect conditions to launch his fintech platform. While others hesitated, he acted swiftly, signing strategic deals and building momentum. His rapid action gave him a competitive edge and proved that progress outweighs perfection.

How to Overcome Overthinking:

- **Set Decision Deadlines**: Avoid over-analysis by setting firm time limits for decisions. Commit to acting within the deadline and move forward with confidence.

- **Progress Over Perfection**: Don't wait for perfect conditions. Start with what you have, take action, and refine along the way. Progress is what truly drives success.

- **Break Big Decisions Into Smaller Ones**: Simplify complexity by focusing on the next actionable step. Tackling smaller pieces makes big decisions more manageable and less intimidating.

3. The Challenge of Maintaining Momentum

"Success is the sum of small efforts, repeated day in and day out."

– Robert Collier

Starting strong is easy; staying consistent is hard. Momentum fades when motivation wanes or setbacks arise. The key to success is **persistence— doing the work even when excitement wears off.**

Story: Nikhil Desai – Staying the Course in the Face of Setbacks

Nikhil's early career was riddled with setbacks, but he never stopped moving forward. By staying focused on his long-term vision and taking consistent action, he became a globally successful corporate trainer. His journey is proof that perseverance creates breakthroughs.

How to Maintain Momentum:

- **Set Daily or Weekly Goals**: Break big your dreams into small, actionable steps. Consistent progress on these smaller goals builds momentum and keeps you moving forward.

- **Celebrate Small Wins**: Every achievement, no matter how small, deserves recognition. Celebrating progress keeps you motivated.

- **Find Accountability**: Partner with a mentor, coach, or accountability buddy who can provide guidance, track your progress, and help you stay on course.

4. Lack of Clarity

"Clarity precedes success."

– Robin Sharma

When goals are vague, actions lack direction. Without clarity, it's easy to feel lost, scattered, or overwhelmed. **Clarity focuses your energy and aligns your efforts with what truly matters.**

Story: Sandeep Mall – Finding Clarity and Transforming His Life

Sandeep struggled with both health and business challenges until he defined crystal-clear goals. By identifying what he wanted—a healthier lifestyle and a thriving business—he took massive, focused action. Clarity became his compass, guiding him toward transformation.

How to Gain Clarity:

- **Ask the Right Questions**: What do you want? Why does it matter? Answering these questions creates focus.

- **Write Down Your Vision**: A written goal feels tangible and actionable.

- **Refine as You Go**: Clarity evolves with action—keep adjusting your vision based on progress.

Summary: Overcoming Obstacles to FRMA

 Success is not the absence of obstacles but the mastery of overcoming them. Here's how to tackle the most common challenges:

1. **Fear of Failure:**
    - Reframe failure as a lesson.
    - Start small to build confidence.
    - Confront worst-case scenarios to diminish fear.

2. **Overthinking:**
    - Set decision deadlines.
    - Prioritize progress over perfection.
    - Break big decisions into smaller steps.

3. **Maintaining Momentum:**
    - Set short-term goals.
    - Celebrate small wins.
    - Find accountability partners.

4. **Lack of Clarity:**
    - Define your "why."
    - Write down clear goals.
    - Refine your vision as you progress.

Actionable Takeaway

Identify one obstacle—whether it's fear, overthinking, momentum loss, or lack of clarity—that's holding you back. Commit to a single strategy from this chapter to overcome it. Take that bold step **this week** and move closer to your goals.

Now that you've learned how to overcome the common obstacles to FRMA, it's time to implement the mantra into your life. In **Chapter 8: The Blueprint for Success**, we'll provide a step-by-step guide to help you embed Focused, Rapid, Massive Action into everything you do, turning dreams into achievements.

THE BLUEPRINT FOR SUCCESS – IMPLEMENTING THE FRMA MANTRA IN YOUR LIFE

*"An idea not coupled with action will never get any
bigger than the brain cell it occupied."*

– Arnold Glasow

You've seen how extraordinary individuals transformed their lives using the **Focused, Rapid, Massive Action (FRMA)** mantra. But knowledge alone isn't enough—true transformation happens when you take that knowledge and **put it into action.**

This chapter is your **step-by-step blueprint** for implementing the FRMA mantra in your life. Think of it as a personal success manual to bridge the gap between dreaming and achieving. It's time to take charge and turn your vision into reality.

1. Start with Clarity – Define Your Vision

*"Clarity is power. The more clear you are about
what you want, the more likely you are to achieve it."*

– Tony Robbins

Without clarity, you're like a ship without a compass—adrift, directionless, and at the mercy of distractions. **Clarity gives you purpose.** It defines what success looks like and helps you channel your energy toward meaningful actions.

Exercise: Craft Your Vision Statement

Take 10 minutes to write down your vision for the next 12 months. Be specific and actionable. Avoid vague goals like "I want to be successful." Instead, define exactly what success means for you:

- **Career:** Increase revenue by 50% and secure three high-profile clients.
- **Health:** Lose 20 pounds and complete a half marathon by December.

Why This Works

A clear vision eliminates ambiguity and provides a concrete target. **When you know what you're aiming for, every step becomes more intentional and aligned.**

2. Focus – Prioritize What Matters Most

"What you focus on expands."

– T. Harv Eker

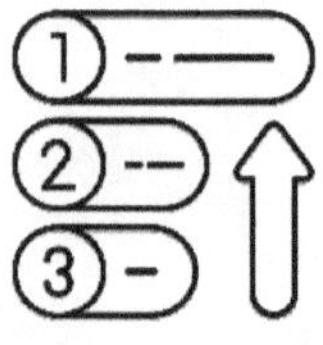

Once you're clear on your vision, the next step is to **laser-focus on high-impact actions**—the critical few tasks that will create the greatest results. Most people spread themselves too thin, trying to do everything. The secret is in **concentrating on what truly moves the needle.**

Exercise: Identify Your High-Impact Actions

Ask yourself: *What are the top three actions that will bring me closest to my vision?* Write them down and prioritize them. Examples:

- **Career:** Reach out to a high-value client, launch a marketing initiative, or finalize a key partnership.
- **Health:** Commit to a workout plan, hire a personal trainer, or make specific improvements to your diet.

Why This Works

Focusing on high-impact actions prevents you from getting lost in busyness. It ensures **you prioritize meaningful progress over activity,** maximizing the return on your efforts.

3. Act Quickly – Develop the Habit of Rapid Action

*"The only difference between success and failure
is the ability to take action."*

– Alexander Graham Bell

Speed is your superpower. The quicker you take action, the faster you build momentum and uncover new opportunities. Don't wait for perfect conditions—they rarely exist. Success comes to those who start now, adapt along the way, and keep pushing forward.

Exercise: Set a 24-Hour Action Deadline

For each high-impact action you listed, commit to taking the first step within the next 24 hours. It doesn't need to be huge—make a call, send an email, or schedule a meeting. The goal is to get moving.

Why This Works

Taking immediate action reduces hesitation and inertia. **Momentum builds confidence, and confidence creates more action.**

4. Go Big – Take Massive Action for Exponential Growth

"Small daily improvements over time lead to stunning results."

– Robin Sharma

While consistency is essential, true breakthroughs happen when you take **bold, decisive actions** that challenge your comfort zone. Taking **massive**

action not only accelerates your growth but also transforms your trajectory.

Exercise: Identify One Bold Move

What's one bold, massive action you can take right now to create a significant shift in your life?

Examples:

- Launching a new product.

- Expanding into a new market.

- Making a radical lifestyle change.

Write it down and commit to taking this bold step within the next 7 days.

Why This Works

Massive action forces you to move beyond incremental progress. It positions you for opportunities and results that small steps can't achieve.

5. Measure and Adjust – Stay Flexible and Refine as You Go

"The key to success is action, and the essential in action is perseverance."

– Sun Yat-sen

No plan is perfect. Success comes from **measuring progress, learning from experience, and refining your strategy** as you go. Flexibility allows you to stay aligned with your vision, even when the path changes.

Exercise: Review and Adjust Weekly

At the end of each week, reflect on your actions and results. Ask yourself:

- What did I accomplish?

- What worked, and what didn't?

- What adjustments do I need to make?

Use these insights to refine your approach and maintain momentum.

Why This Works

Regular reflection keeps you on track and ensures continuous improvement. **It's not about avoiding mistakes; it's about learning and adapting.**

Summary: The Blueprint for Implementing FRMA

1. **Clarity:** Define your vision for the next 12 months. Specific goals provide direction and purpose, making it easier to stay on track.

2. **Focus:** Identify high-impact actions and eliminate distractions to maximize your effectiveness.

3. **Rapid Action:** Commit to taking the first step within 24 hours to build momentum.

4. **Massive Action:** Take bold, decisive actions that create exponential growth and push you closer to your vision.

5. **Measure and Adjust:** Reflect weekly to evaluate progress. Use what you learn to refine your approach and stay aligned with your goals.

Actionable Takeaway

Right now, take 10 minutes to:

1. Write down your vision for the next 12 months.

2. Identify the top three high-impact actions that will move you closer to that vision.

3. Commit to taking the first step within 24 hours.

4. Identify one bold move you'll take within the next 7 days—and go all in.

Next Step: Chapter 9 – Staying the Course: Maintaining Momentum

Momentum is the lifeblood of sustained success. In the next chapter, we'll explore how to maintain the energy and commitment needed to make FRMA a permanent part of your life.

STAYING THE COURSE – MAINTAINING MOMENTUM

*"Success is not about perfection, it's about consistency.
Keep showing up, keep doing the work."*

– Dwayne Johnson

Starting strong with **Focused, Rapid, Massive Action (FRMA)** is the first step. **True success lies in maintaining that momentum over time.** Many people begin their journeys with enthusiasm, only to falter when motivation fades or obstacles arise.

The secret to achieving long-term success isn't about occasional bursts of effort—it's about **persistent, consistent action.** In this chapter, we'll explore how to build habits, create sustainable systems, and develop resilience so you can stay on track and keep moving forward, no matter what challenges arise.

1. Consistency Over Motivation

*"It's not what we do once in a while that shapes our lives.
It's what we do consistently."*

– Tony Robbins

Motivation is a great starter, but it's fleeting. When it disappears, you need something more powerful to keep you going—**consistency.** The most successful people aren't driven by motivation alone; they're powered by habits and routines that keep them moving forward, even on tough days.

Story: Nikhil Desai – The Power of Showing Up Daily

Early in his career, Nikhil Desai faced countless setbacks. Yet, he refused to let those challenges derail him. Instead of waiting for motivation, he relied on **consistent daily effort.** He showed up, did the work, and over time, this commitment transformed him into a globally successful corporate trainer.

How to Stay Consistent When Motivation Fades:

- **Build Routines:** Establish daily habits aligned with your goals to simplify decisions and ensure steady progress, as Nikhil did with disciplined time management.

- **Set Micro Goals:** Divide big goals into small, achievable steps. Each win fuels momentum.

- **Create Accountability:** Seek mentor or accountability partner to ensure you stay on track.

2. Embrace the Dip – Pushing Through Tough Times

"Most people give up just before they're about to achieve success. They quit on the one-yard line."

– Ross Perot

Every journey hits a **dip**—a period where progress slows, obstacles multiply, and self-doubt creeps in. The dip is where most people give up, but it's also where real growth happens. Those who push through the dip emerge stronger, more resilient, and closer to their goals.

Story: Gaurav Jain – Pushing Through the Dip

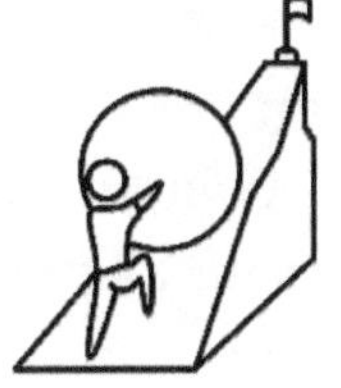

When Gaurav Jain launched his business, the initial excitement fueled rapid progress. However, he faced tough challenges—clients were harder to secure, and deals took longer to close. Instead of quitting, Gaurav embraced the dip, stayed consistent, and eventually turned his struggles into success. His persistence paid off, building a thriving business.

How to Push Through the Dip:

- **Reconnect with Your 'Why':** Reflect on your core purpose. Why did you embark on this journey? What's at stake if you quit?

- **Break It Down:** Simplify the challenge by focusing on the next actionable step instead of feeling overwhelmed by the entire picture.

- **Celebrate Progress:** Success is rarely linear. Recognize and celebrate even the smallest milestones to keep your motivation alive.

3. Stay Aligned with Your Vision

"Where there is no vision, there is no hope."

– George Washington Carver

Over time, it's easy to drift away from your original vision, losing focus and momentum. Staying connected to your vision keeps you motivated and ensures that every action aligns with your ultimate goals.

Story: Sandeep Mall – Staying True to His Vision

Sandeep Mall's personal and professional transformations weren't just about numbers—they were about staying true to a **clear, compelling vision** for his life. That vision served as his anchor, guiding him through challenges and keeping him focused on the bigger picture.

How to Stay Aligned with Your Vision:

- **Review Your Vision Regularly:** Take time weekly or monthly to revisit your goals and ensure they remain top of mind.

- **Visualize Success:** Spend a few minutes daily imagining yourself achieving your goals. Visualization strengthens your connection to your vision.

- **Adapt as Needed:** Your vision can evolve as you grow. Adjust your goals while ensuring they remain aligned with your purpose.

✦✦✦

4. Build a Strong Support System

"Surround yourself with only people who are going to lift you higher."

– Oprah Winfrey

Success is never a solo journey. Behind every great achievement is a network of mentors, peers, and supporters who provide guidance, encouragement, and accountability. A strong support system can lift you up during tough times and keep you grounded when things are going well.

Story: Bhavik Vasa – Leveraging His Network for Support

Bhavik Vasa didn't achieve success in fintech on his own. He leaned on a network of mentors and peers for feedback and encouragement. This support system gave him the clarity and resilience needed to push through challenges and achieve his goals.

How to Build a Support System:

- **Find Accountability Partners:** Choose people who will hold you to your commitments and provide honest feedback.

- **Seek Mentors:** Learn from those who have already achieved what you aspire to. Their guidance is invaluable.

- **Join Communities:** Engage with like-minded individuals who share your goals. Communities provide energy, resources, and motivation.

Summary: Staying the Course and Maintaining Momentum

1. **Consistency Over Motivation:** Develop habits, set micro-goals, and use accountability to stay consistent, even when motivation fades.

2. **Embrace the Dip:** Push through tough times by reconnecting with your purpose, breaking challenges into small steps, and celebrating progress.

3. **Stay Aligned with Your Vision:** Regularly review your goals, visualize success, and adapt your vision as you grow.

4. **Build a Strong Support System:** Surround yourself with mentors, accountability partners, and a supportive community.

Actionable Takeaway

Take 10 minutes today to:

1. Design a simple daily routine that keeps you consistent.

2. Reach out to one person—a mentor, friend, or peer—who can hold you accountable to your goals.

3. Write down one strategy to help you push through the next "dip" you encounter.

Next Step: Chapter 10 – The Impact of FRMA: Real Transformation Stories

In the next chapter, we'll showcase real-life transformations of people who applied the FRMA mantra. These stories will inspire you to take bold action and prove that extraordinary success is possible when you commit to Focused, Rapid, Massive Action.

THE IMPACT OF FRMA – REAL TRANSFORMATION STORIES

"Action is the foundational key to all success."

– Pablo Picasso

You've learned about the transformative power of **Focused, Rapid, Massive Action (FRMA)**. Now, it's time to see how these principles play out in real life. This chapter dives into the stories of 10 extraordinary individuals who embraced FRMA to overcome challenges and achieve breakthrough success.

These aren't just inspiring tales—they're blueprints for action. Each story proves that when you commit to FRMA, you unlock opportunities you never thought possible. Let these examples ignite your own journey of transformation.

1. Alok Bector: Innovating His Way to Success

In the fiercely competitive pharmaceutical equipment industry, Alok faced giants. Instead of competing on size, he focused on **relentless innovation**. By committing to improving every product, Alok turned his company into an industry leader.

Key Transformation Insight:

Focus on innovation.

Focused action on one critical area can elevate you above even the toughest competition.

2. Bhavik Vasa: Seizing Opportunities in Fintech

Returning to India from Silicon Valley, Bhavik saw fintech as a wide-open frontier. While others hesitated, he took **rapid action** — launching a platform and forging critical partnerships. His decisiveness secured him a first-mover advantage.

Key Transformation Insight:

Rapid action is your competitive edge.

Bhavik's speed positioned him as an industry leader even before competitors could react.

3. Deepika Narayan Bhardwaj: Fighting for Justice Through Bold Action

Faced with personal challenges, Deepika took **massive action** to become a filmmaker and activist. Her fearless commitment to exposing injustices sparked a national movement for legal reform.

Key Transformation Insight:

Massive action creates lasting change.

Bold steps in the face of adversity can create ripples that transform lives.

4. Uday Sanghavi: Disrupting an Industry with Precision Focus

In the stagnant packaging machinery industry, Uday zeroed in on **custom automation solutions**. By narrowing his focus, he outperformed larger competitors and built a reputation for expertise.

Key Transformation Insight:

Focus creates differentiation.

Honing in on a niche allowed Uday to disrupt a stagnant industry and achieve exponential growth.

5. Nilesh Karandikar: Building an Empire Through Consistent Focus

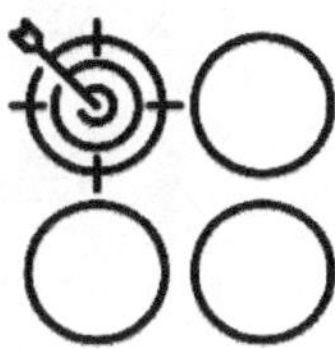

Nilesh avoided spreading himself thin and chose to specialize in **industrial manipulators**. His deep expertise and consistent focus turned his business into a leader in the manufacturing sector.

Key Transformation Insight:

Consistency and focus build expertise.

Commitment to one niche creates sustainable, long-term success.

6. Sandeep Mall: Transforming Health and Business Through Bold Decisions

Facing stagnation, Sandeep embraced **massive action** by overhauling his health and business simultaneously. Bold decisions led to dramatic improvements in every aspect of his life.

Key Transformation Insight:

Massive action leads to total transformation.

Taking bold steps can create breakthroughs in both personal and professional spheres.

7. Gaurav Jain: Launching a Business with Speed and Precision

Leaving a corporate job, Gaurav knew speed was his advantage. He launched his business swiftly, secured clients early, and built momentum that sustained his growth.

Key Transformation Insight:

Momentum starts with rapid action.

Quick, decisive action laid the foundation for Gaurav's thriving business.

8. Pawan Pamecha: Scaling Globally Through Bold Moves

Pawan turned his local business into a global success by taking **bold, decisive actions**. His willingness to embrace international opportunities led to exponential growth.

Key Transformation Insight:

Massive action leads to exponential growth.

Scaling globally requires bold, fearless decisions.

9. Madhusudanan R: Pioneering Fintech with Rapid Action

Madhusudanan didn't wait for perfect conditions. By moving quickly to launch his fintech platform and form partnerships, he established himself as a pioneer.

Key Transformation Insight: Speed is a first-mover advantage.

Rapid action positions you as a leader before others even begin.

10. Nikhil Desai: Turning Setbacks into Opportunities with Focused Action

Despite setbacks, Nikhil focused on improving his skills and achieving his goals. Over time, his persistence turned him into a globally recognized corporate trainer.

Key Transformation Insight:

Focused action turns setbacks into opportunities.

Staying focused through challenges leads to extraordinary results.

The Impact of FRMA: Lessons from Real Achievers

The journeys of these 10 achievers showcase the **transformative power of FRMA:**

1. **Focus** creates clarity and direction, enabling mastery in your niche.

2. **Rapid Action** builds momentum and opens doors others overlook.

3. **Massive Action** drives exponential growth and long-term impact.

These individuals didn't wait for the perfect moment—they made it happen. Their transformations are proof that **Focused, Rapid, Massive Action** can unlock extraordinary success in any area of life.

Actionable Takeaway

 Identify one area of your life where you've been holding back. Ask yourself:

- What is one **bold, massive action** I can take today that would create a breakthrough?

Please write it down, commit to it, and take the first step immediately.

Your transformation begins with action.

Next Step: Conclusion – Becoming Unstoppable with FRMA

In the final chapter, we'll tie everything together, showing you how to embed the FRMA mantra into your daily life to create unstoppable momentum. This isn't just about achieving goals—it's about building a life of purpose, passion, and extraordinary results.

CONCLUSION – YOUR JOURNEY BEGINS NOW

"The future depends on what you do today."

– Mahatma Gandhi

As you reach the final pages of this book, I want you to feel more than inspired—I want you to feel unstoppable. The strategies, stories, and exercises you've encountered are your blueprint for transformation. They are not reserved for the privileged few; they are for anyone ready to take bold, decisive action.

But let's be clear: Inspiration alone doesn't lead to success. **Action does.** Focused, Rapid, Massive Action (FRMA) is the key to unlocking your potential. The achievers you've read about didn't wait for perfect circumstances—they created their opportunities. Now it's your turn.

1. Reflect on What You've Learned

Take a moment to reflect on the lessons and stories in this book. From the **power of focus** to the **momentum of rapid action** and the **breakthroughs of massive action**, you now hold the tools to transform your life.

Consider the journeys of Alok, Bhavik, Deepika, and others. They faced uncertainty and setbacks, just like you. They could have waited for the "right" moment—but they didn't. They acted.

Now ask yourself:

- What goals have I been putting off?
- Where have I been holding back, waiting for perfect conditions?

The truth is, **the right time is now.** There will never be a perfect moment. Success is about what you do today, not what you plan for someday.

2. Commit to Focused, Rapid, Massive Action

The road ahead won't be easy, but it will be worth it. As you begin this next chapter of your life, commit fully to the FRMA mantra:

- **Focus**: Eliminate distractions and channel your energy towards what truly matters.

- **Act Rapidly**: Don't wait for permission or perfection. Seize opportunities now.

- **Take Massive Action**: Be bold. Step out of your comfort zone. The greatest rewards lie beyond fear.

3. Create Your Personal Action Plan

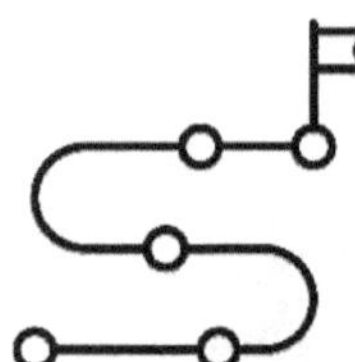

It's time to turn inspiration into action. Follow these steps to implement FRMA immediately:

1. **Define Your Vision**: What do you want to achieve in the next 12 months? Be specific.

   Example: "I will double my income and launch a new product line by December."

2. **Identify Your High-Impact Actions**: List three actions that will bring you closer to your vision.

   Example: Reach out to five potential clients, finalize a marketing plan, or secure funding.

3. **Set a 24-Hour Action Deadline**: For each action, commit to taking the first step within 24 hours.

4. **Plan Your Massive Action**: Identify one bold, transformative move you'll make within the next seven days.

Example: Launch your business, propose a game-changing idea, or take a major personal risk.

5. **Track Your Progress**: Use a daily or weekly tracker to measure your results. Celebrate wins and adjust as needed.

4. Your Journey is Unique, But You're Not Alone

Success is personal, but it doesn't have to be a lonely journey. Surround yourself with mentors, peers, and supporters who believe in your vision. Build a **support system** that lifts you when challenges arise.

Remember, the achievers you've read about in this book weren't born with all the answers. They relied on consistency, resilience, and the strength of their networks. Success doesn't happen overnight, but it does happen for those who refuse to quit.

5. Final Word of Encouragement

The most powerful lesson I hope you take from this book is this: **You have the power to create change.** You don't need permission. You don't need to wait. Everything you need to succeed is already within you.

"Your life does not get better by chance; it gets better by change."

– Jim Rohn

Success isn't a distant dream; it's a series of bold decisions and consistent actions. Every step you take brings you closer to your vision.

So go out there and take **Focused, Rapid, Massive Action**.

Start today.

Actionable Takeaway

Before you close this book:

1.   Take 10 minutes to write your **FRMA Action Plan:**

- Your vision for the next 12 months.

- Three high-impact actions you'll take immediately.

- One bold, massive action you'll commit to within seven days.

2.   Commit to taking your first step within the next **24 hours**.

This is your moment. Your journey begins now.

INTRODUCTION TO THE FRMA BIG ACHIEVERS – THEIR STORIES AND KEY LEARNINGS

 At the heart of this book are not just principles, but real, lived experiences of those who dared to take **Focused, Rapid, Massive Action (FRMA)** and completely transformed their lives and businesses. These aren't theories. These are true stories of individuals who faced obstacles, embraced risk, and emerged as extraordinary achievers.

The ten remarkable individuals you're about to meet didn't wait for ideal conditions. **They acted when others hesitated.** They made bold decisions when uncertainty loomed. They pushed through challenges that would have stopped most people in their tracks. Whether overcoming personal struggles, capturing business opportunities in a competitive market, or making high-stakes decisions under pressure, they applied the FRMA mantra in powerful ways.

These stories **prove one undeniable truth:** *Success is not reserved for the few—it's available to those who act decisively and with focus.* These achievers come from different walks of life, but all share one key trait: the determination to push beyond limits, adapt quickly, and act boldly, without waiting for the perfect time or circumstances.

In these pages, you'll find the blueprints of transformation. **You'll see how massive success is fueled by focused effort, quick, calculated decisions, and actions that may feel uncomfortable but lead to exponential growth.** From business expansions and personal reinventions to conquering new markets and turning adversity into opportunity—**these are real-life stories of triumph against the odds.**

As you read their journeys, ask yourself: **What's holding me back from taking my bold action?** Their stories aren't just to inspire you—they're your **call to action**. These achievers didn't wait. **They acted, they failed, they learned—and they won.** And so can you.

Take their lessons to heart. Let their stories **fuel your journey** toward greatness. This is your proof that **no dream is too big, and no challenge too great**, when you embrace the power of Focused, Rapid, Massive Action.

✦✦✦

####

Story 1: Alok Bector – Building a Legacy Through Focused, Rapid, Massive Action

Alok Bector's journey is nothing short of remarkable. From humble beginnings working in a small workshop to becoming a major player in the pharmaceutical equipment industry, his story demonstrates the sheer power of **Focused, Rapid, Massive Action (FRMA)** in overcoming obstacles and achieving extraordinary success.

Early Struggles and Breakthroughs

Alok didn't follow a conventional path. Dissatisfied with formal education, he joined his family's fledgling business, Bechtochem, a small company his father started in the early 1980s. Starting with menial tasks—polishing vessels and typing quotes—Alok worked under immense economic and social pressure. However, his early marriage became a pivotal moment, igniting a sense of responsibility that would fuel his relentless drive.

Working 20-hour days with no clear vision at first, Alok's relentless effort laid the foundation for future breakthroughs. His journey demonstrates that **relentless action, even without a defined roadmap, can spark massive growth.**

Focused Action: Innovating to Stay Ahead

Alok's success stemmed from a sharp focus on constant innovation. Rather than competing solely on price or scale, he concentrated on being better and different—introducing technological advances like microprocessor-based control panels, well ahead of the competition. His vision was not about short-term gains; it was about **creating a legacy of lasting impact.**

A key turning point came with a strategic partnership with Ross Mixing, a U.S.-based company, further elevating Bechtochem's reputation. Alok's focus wasn't just on product innovation; he also nurtured **deep, trust-based relationships** with customers and partners, understanding that **relationships, not just technology, sustain long-term success.**

Alok's Advice:

> *"Relationships in business last longer than technology.*
> *You can have the best machines, but it's the trust you*
> *build that keeps the doors open."*

Rapid Action: Seizing Opportunities with Speed

Alok's swift decision-making was another pivotal factor in his success. In 1988, recognizing Gujarat's Ankleshwar region as an emerging hub for the pharmaceutical industry, he quickly relocated his factory there—a move that would later prove essential to his company's expansion.

His agility was further tested when Procter & Gamble approached him with a specialized coating process requirement. Alok didn't hesitate. He set up a factory in just three months, meeting P&G's needs and securing a long-term contract that would significantly boost his company's growth.

Speed creates a competitive advantage and Alok exemplified this principle. By acting decisively, he seized opportunities that others might have overlooked, proving that success favors those who move with purpose and urgency.

Alok's Advice:

> *"The right opportunities don't wait for you.*
> *Speed matters—either you jump in or someone else will."*

Massive Action: Bold Moves for Big Gains

Throughout his career, Alok consistently took **bold, massive action.** Whether it was securing large loans for expansion, making high-risk investments, or selling a 51% stake in his company to a German partner, he demonstrated the courage to act when others hesitated. His decision to invest in robotics and automation in 2012—despite immediate losses—showed his unwavering belief in long-term gains.

Even when his colleagues and family resisted his decision to sell a majority stake in his business, Alok stayed the course. This move allowed Bechtochem to grow globally, positioning it as a leading player in the industry.

Alok understood that **playing it safe leads to mediocrity.** His willingness to take significant risks, even when the returns weren't immediately visible, ultimately paid off and propelled his business to new heights.

Alok's Advice:

> *"If you want to grow big, you have to make bold moves.*
> *Playing it safe is a sure way to stay small."*

Key Lessons from Alok Bector's Journey

1. **Innovation Comes from Focus** – Alok's unwavering focus on innovation kept his company relevant and ahead of the competition. His commitment to improvement and forging key partnerships ensured consistent progress and sustained growth.

2. **Seize Opportunities with Speed** – Alok's rapid decision-making, such as relocating to Gujarat and securing key contracts, gave him a vital competitive edge. His readiness to act swiftly, even in high-risk scenarios, allowed him to capture opportunities others would have missed.

3. **Take Bold, Massive Action** – Alok never hesitated to take massive, bold risks, from high-stakes investments to selling a stake in his company. These fearless moves not only transformed his business but also positioned him for long-term success.

4. **Stay the Course** – Alok's persistence, especially in the face of adversity, was key to his long-term gains. He understood that **short-term sacrifices lead to long-term rewards**, and he remained committed to his vision, even when others doubted him.

Alok's story serves as a powerful reminder that **focused action, swift decisions, and bold moves are essential for building a lasting legacy**. His journey inspires us to take initiative, embrace risks, and stay committed to what truly matters.

Story 2: Nikhil Desai – From Humble Beginnings to Global Impact

Nikhil Desai's journey is a shining example of the transformative power of **Focused, Rapid, Massive Action (FRMA)**. From his modest upbringing in a middle-class family, Nikhil rose to become an internationally acclaimed motivational speaker and corporate trainer. His story proves that with relentless focus, timely decisions, and bold actions, even the most challenging dreams can be realized.

Early Struggles and Formative Moments

Growing up in a family that valued integrity and hard work over material wealth, Nikhil learned early that he would need to earn everything through effort and persistence. A pivotal moment came during his school days when he was terrified of giving a speech for his house captain election. He almost quit—but with encouragement from his parents and the help of a coach, Nikhil delivered the speech and won the election. This experience laid the foundation for his future as a motivational speaker.

Nikhil's challenges didn't end there. While pursuing an MBA in the U.S.,he overcame financial hurdles, secured an RBI permit, and balanced work while studying. His determination to succeed in a foreign land and repay debts instilled a resilient work ethic that would shape his future success.

Focused Action: Relentless Pursuit of Purpose

Nikhil's career as a trainer and motivational speaker was born out of a deep desire to **help people reach their potential.** After attending life-skills programs in New York, he realized these tools could have a significant impact back in India. His focus became clear: **help people manage time, improve productivity, and lead more fulfilling lives.**

The early years were difficult. Nikhil struggled to find clients willing to pay for his services, and for three years, he conducted free programs, honing his skills and building his network. His unwavering focus on "making a difference" (MAD, as he calls it) kept him going through the toughest times. Finally, after three long years, Nikhil secured his first major client, launching his paid career and fulfilling his mission to make a lasting impact on others' lives.

Nikhil's Advice:

"If you don't believe in your purpose,
nobody else will. Your focus will always drive your results."

Rapid Action: Adapting to Change at Lightning Speed

One of Nikhil's defining traits is his ability to act quickly in the face of change. A powerful example of this came during the COVID-19 pandemic. When in-person training sessions were canceled due to lockdowns, Nikhil was faced with a choice: break his 30-year streak of never canceling a program or adapting. **Without hesitation**, he moved his sessions online—something he had never done before.

Within days, Nikhil transitioned to virtual training and continued to deliver programs on time management, leadership, and stress management. Over two years, he conducted **105 online sessions**, expanding his reach globally to audiences in Africa and the U.S. His rapid adaptation not only kept his streak alive but also opened new international opportunities.

Nikhil's Advice:

*"When you're faced with a challenge, your first move should be forward—***speed over hesitation*** is key."*

Massive Action: Bold Moves to Multiply Impact

Nikhil's career is defined by bold decisions that multiplied his impact exponentially. Initially, he worked with small groups of 20-25 people, but he soon realized that if he truly wanted to **make a massive difference**, he needed to reach larger audiences. This led him to pivot toward motivational speaking, allowing him to address hundreds of people in shorter, high-impact sessions.

This bold decision enabled Nikhil to scale his career dramatically. Today, he conducts multiple sessions a day, both in-person and online, impacting thousands of lives globally. His decisive action maximized his time, expanded his reach, and multiplied the number of individuals he could inspire and empower.

Nikhil's Advice:

"To achieve big, you need to think big.
Stop playing small—massive impact requires massive action."

Key Lessons from Nikhil Desai's Journey

1. **Persistence Pays Off** – Nikhil's unwavering focus on his mission, even during years of setbacks, demonstrates that **persistence leads to breakthroughs**. His commitment to making a difference kept him on track, even when financial success seemed distant.

2. **Adapt Quickly or Fall Behind** – Nikhil's rapid adaptation to online programs during the pandemic illustrates the importance of speed and flexibility. His ability to make swift decisions helped him **thrive when many others struggled**.

3. **Think Big, Act Boldly** – Nikhil's shift from small training sessions to large motivational talks was a game-changer for his career. By **thinking big and taking bold action**, he was able to scale his impact and achieve massive success.

4. **Learn Continuously** – Nikhil's dedication to lifelong learning has kept him relevant and effective in his field for over three decades. His success is proof that **continuous growth is essential for long-term impact.**

Nikhil Desai's story serves as a powerful reminder that **persistence, speed, and decisive action are crucial for overcoming challenges and creating lasting impact.** His journey inspires us to **act decisively, think ambitiously, and remain steadfast in our purpose.**

Story 3: Uday Sanghavi – Building Success from Dreams to Reality

Uday Sanghavi's journey is a remarkable example of how **Focused, Rapid, and Massive Action (FRMA)** can turn dreams into reality. From growing up in a joint family with a small business to building an international enterprise, Uday's story is one of **persistence, bold decision-making**, and a relentless focus on long-term goals.

Early Dreams and Overcoming Challenges

Born into a family where business was a way of life, Uday's fascination with machines began early as he watched his father run a small machine workshop. But Uday's dream went beyond just making spare parts—he envisioned building cutting-edge technology-based products under a brand name. His desire to transform the family business into something larger pushed him to aim for **something bigger** than the status quo.

However, the journey was not without its hurdles. Uday faced significant challenges, including **competing with established**

brands and earning the trust of customers despite being a small company with ambitious goals. Yet, his family's encouragement to "choose between a crowded local train or a comfortable Mercedes" motivated him to keep pushing forward.

Key Advice from Uday:

- "The comfort zone is where dreams die. If you want something bigger, you have to be willing to push beyond the familiar."

Focused Action: Creating Breakthroughs with a Singular Vision

Uday's success can be attributed to his **laser-sharp focus** on a singular vision. A pivotal moment came when he decided to move beyond producing mechanical machines to developing **advanced electronic packing machines**. He identified the opportunity that foreign-made machines with electronic controls were more accurate and more efficient. Uday committed himself to creating a similar machine, offering superior technology at a competitive price.

This breakthrough **differentiated his company in a competitive market** and proved to be a pivotal moment in his career. Uday's unwavering focus on innovation allowed him to **leap ahead of the competition** and establish his business as a leader in the packing machinery space. His continued focus on setting new goals and concentrating efforts on **one key task at a time** played a vital role in his steady growth.

Key Advice from Uday:

- "It's not just about working hard; it's about working hard on the right things—**focus defines the scale** of your success."

Rapid Action: Seizing Opportunities with Confidence

A key factor in Uday's success is his ability to **make swift decisions** and seize opportunities as they arise. When a client in Orissa requested a machine that could cool gas without using water – a novel challenge for his company – Uday did not hesitate. Instead of turning down the challenge, he took immediate action, assuring the client that his company could deliver. Within a short time, they developed the **air cooler**, which became an important product line for his business.

This ability to **act quickly** not only secured new business but also **established Uday's reputation for innovation**. Throughout his career, Uday has consistently acted fast when opportunities presented themselves, understanding that waiting too long could mean **missing out** on significant growth.

Key Advice from Uday:

- "Opportunities are like trains—you either **jump on** or watch them pass. Waiting too long means **missing out**."

Massive Action: Taking Bold Steps for Growth

Uday's career is filled with **bold moves** that have defined his success. One of the most impactful decisions was his choice to **leave the family business** and start his venture. Despite having only, a 20% share of the family business, Uday's vision pushed him to **create something on his terms**. This decision allowed him the freedom to pursue his goals more aggressively and ultimately led to greater success.

Another bold move was Uday's **expansion into international markets**, particularly Malaysia. Despite facing fierce competition within the Indian market, he proactively pursued international growth, undertaking substantial projects that entailed significant investment and operational risks. His calculated risk paid off, allowing him to establish a foothold in global markets and boost his company's reputation.

In addition to business expansion, Uday took massive action in **upgrading his company's processes**, implementing systems like SAP, and professionalizing his workforce. These moves set his company up for **long-term sustainability** and operational efficiency, proving that **massive action creates exponential growth**.

Key Advice from Uday:

- "If you don't take massive steps forward, you'll always stay where you are. **Success demands bold, decisive action.**"

Key Lessons from Uday Sanghavi's Journey

1. **Dream Big, Act Boldly** – Uday's journey shows the power of **dreaming beyond the ordinary** and taking **bold steps** to achieve those dreams. From wanting to move beyond spare parts to developing advanced technology, Uday's willingness to take risks fuelled his success.

2. **Seize Opportunities Quickly** – Uday's ability to **act swiftly** on critical opportunities, such as developing air coolers, demonstrates that **speed** is often the key to securing business and gaining a competitive edge.

3. **Focus on Long-Term Goals** – Uday's commitment to his **long-term vision** kept him on track even when facing challenges. Whether developing new products or expanding internationally, his **focus on the bigger picture** ensured his success.

4. **Calculated Risks Lead to Growth** – From stepping away from the family business to venturing into international markets, Uday's journey shows that **taking calculated risks** is essential for growth and long-term success.

Uday Sanghavi's remarkable journey serves as a powerful testament to the fact that dreams necessitate bold action, swift decision-making, and an unwavering focus on long-term objectives. His journey inspires us to take risks, move fast, and never lose sight of our vision, even when the challenges seem insurmountable.

Story 4: Pawan Pamecha – From Local Entrepreneur to Global Leader

Pawan Pamecha's story is a powerful testament to the transformative power of **Focused, Rapid, and Massive Action (FRMA)** in building a global empire. From humble beginnings in a small local business to becoming a global leader in the furniture industry, Pawan's journey is one of **persistence, seizing opportunities**, and **bold decision-making**.

Early Beginnings and Facing Adversity

Pawan's entrepreneurial journey began in the early 1980s when he started a small furniture manufacturing business in India. The local market was challenging—stiff competition, slim margins, and financial pressure made growth difficult. Despite these obstacles, Pawan's **vision extended far beyond** his current scope. He wasn't just focused on surviving—he was determined to **expand** and eventually tap into international markets.

His early years were filled with struggles, but Pawan's **unwavering belief** in his vision kept him going. Through relentless work and dedication, he started laying the foundation for something much bigger.

Key Advice from Pawan:

- "If you believe in your vision, **persistence is your greatest tool**. The road may be tough, but the destination is worth every challenge."

Focused Action: Mastering Innovation and Market Expansion

A pivotal moment in Pawan's journey arrived when he recognized that competing within the local market wouldn't lead to the success he envisioned. Rather than engaging in a price war with local competitors, Pawan strategically shifted his focus towards **importing high-end furniture designs from Europe and Southeast Asia**. This strategic pivot was a **game-changer**.

By focusing on offering **unique, high-quality products**, Pawan carved out a distinct niche for his business. His emphasis on quality, innovation, and customer service positioned him as a leader in a competitive market, allowing his company to **grow rapidly**. This move from local manufacturing to global importation not only expanded his reach but also set the stage for future success.

Key Advice from Pawan:

- "The key to growth isn't just working harder—it's **working smarter**. Focus on what sets you apart and build from there."

Rapid Action: Taking Advantage of Policy Changes

Pawan's success was also driven by his ability to **act quickly** in response to external opportunities. One of the most significant turning points came in the 1990s, when the Indian government introduced the **Open General License (OGL) policy**, which made it easier for businesses to import goods.

While others hesitated, Pawan saw a massive opportunity and **moved swiftly**. He quickly shifted his business model to capitalize on the new policy, becoming one of the first to import furniture from Europe. His ability to act rapidly gave him a **first-mover advantage**, and within a short time, he became one of India's largest furniture importers.

Key Advice from Pawan:

- "Opportunities don't wait. If you see a window of growth, don't hesitate—**jump in and figure out the rest along the way**."

Massive Action: Scaling Internationally

Arguably, the boldest and most transformative step in Pawan's journey was his decision to **expand internationally**. After years of importing, Pawan saw another opportunity—**exporting**. He diligently cultivated relationships with global suppliers and buyers, ultimately establishing export channels to over **90 countries worldwide.**

This massive action wasn't without risk. Pawan had to invest heavily in **infrastructure, logistics, and partnerships** to make international expansion a reality. Despite encountering regulatory hurdles and financial pressures, his belief in his vision drove him forward. Today, his company is a major player in the global furniture market, exporting to **Europe, Southeast Asia, and the Middle East.**

Pawan's bold moves and willingness to take risks transformed his business from a **local operation** into a **global powerhouse.**

Key Advice from Pawan:

- "To achieve massive success, you need to take **massive action**. You can't be afraid of big moves—they are what separates the successful from the ordinary."

Key Lessons from Pawan Pamecha's Journey

1. **Persistence Leads to Breakthroughs** – Pawan's unwavering persistence in the face of adversity is a key takeaway. Even when faced with financial struggles and stiff competition, he never wavered from his vision, and his persistence ultimately paid off.

2. **Focus on Differentiation** – Pawan's decision to shift from local manufacturing to **importing high-quality furniture** gave him a **competitive edge**. By focusing on providing unique products, he was able to stand out in a saturated market and grow his business.

3. **Act Quickly on Opportunities** – Pawan's ability to **seize opportunities rapidly**, especially in response to the OGL policy, set him apart from competitors. His quick decision-making allowed him to capitalize on market changes and gain a **first-mover advantage.**

4. **Take Bold, Massive Action** – Pawan's **international expansion** was the turning point in his business. By taking **calculated risks** and scaling his operations globally, he transformed his company into a **global market leader**.

Pawan Pamecha's story is a compelling reminder that **massive success requires bold actions, quick decisions**, and a relentless focus on growth. His journey from a small local business to a global leader serves as an inspiration to entrepreneurs everywhere: **when you act decisively, stay persistent, and take massive steps forward, the world becomes your market.**

Story 5: Gaurav Jain – Embracing Risks and Building Success Through Focused, Rapid, Massive Action

Gaurav Jain's journey exemplifies the transformative power of **Focused, Rapid, and Massive Action (FRMA)**. From being an average student to becoming a successful entrepreneur, Gaurav's story highlights how taking bold steps, acting quickly, and maintaining laser-sharp focus can lead to extraordinary achievements.

Early Days: From an Average Student to a Gold Medalist

Gaurav's early life was defined by being an average student from a middle-class family. However, everything changed when he decided to pursue his **Chartered Accountancy (CA)** and later his MBA. During his rigorous CA final examinations, Gaurav underwent a dramatic transformation in his mindset. He embarked on a period of intense self-isolation, **dedicating 12-13 hours daily to rigorous study with unwavering focus.**

This period of intense focus paid off. Not only did Gaurav pass his exams, but he secured a **gold medal**—a remarkable achievement for someone who had not excelled academically in the past. This experience taught him a vital lesson: **success doesn't require brilliance—it demands absolute focus and dedication.**

Key Advice from Gaurav:

- "Success is not about brilliance. It's about **focus**. If you can focus intensely, you can achieve anything, no matter where you start."

Focused Action: A Life-Long Strategy

Focus became the cornerstone of Gaurav's success. Whether in his studies, his corporate career, or later entrepreneurial ventures, he has consistently observed that **sustained focus on a single goal** yields extraordinary results. However, Gaurav stresses the importance of **focusing on the right things**. "You may focus on the wrong thing, and the results may still not come in your favor. It's important to figure out what to focus on and then commit to it," he explains.

In his **14-year corporate career**, Gaurav consistently honed his skills, eventually becoming a Vice President. But his ultimate focus was always on building a foundation for **future entrepreneurial success**. This long-term vision led him to take the bold step of leaving the corporate world to start his own business.

Key Advice from Gaurav:

- "Your focus should be like a **laser beam**—clear and unwavering. But make sure it's pointed at the right target."

Rapid Action: Taking Calculated Risks and Moving Fast

One of the defining traits of Gaurav's journey is his ability to take **rapid action** when the moment calls for it. At the age of 42, Gaurav made the bold decision to leave his well-paying corporate job as Vice President to pursue **entrepreneurship**. While his peers were settling into stable careers, Gaurav felt an undeniable pull toward his entrepreneurial dream—a dream he had nurtured since the age of 18.

Within **three months** of leaving his job, Gaurav had established his own office, hired a small team, and secured **15 clients** —an impressive feat in the **B2B space**. His ability to make swift decisions, even amid uncertainty, allowed him to scale his business quickly. By the end of his second year, his company had generated **$18 million in revenue**—a testament to his quick decision-making and willingness to take risks.

Key Advice from Gaurav:

- "The faster you move, the quicker you'll learn. Sometimes, waiting for the perfect moment means **missing the opportunity** entirely."

Massive Action: Scaling a New Venture from Scratch

Gaurav's boldest move came when he left a **secure, well-paying corporate job** to pursue his entrepreneurial aspirations. This massive action required not only courage but also a clear strategy for growth. Within just **two years**, Gaurav had built a team, secured major clients, and generated impressive revenue—all while navigating the challenges of being a **first-generation entrepreneur**.

Operating in a **highly competitive B2B environment** with over 40 players, Gaurav managed to carve out a **niche** for his company. His willingness to take massive action—by hiring the right people, investing in marketing, and developing products—propelled him towards rapid success. This bold approach to business growth was the driving force behind his success, allowing him to **stand out** and thrive in a crowded market.

Key Advice from Gaurav:

- Small steps might keep you safe, but **big, bold moves** will change your life. **Massive action** is the key to massive success.

Key Lessons from Gaurav Jain's Journey

1. **Focus and Commitment Lead to Breakthroughs** – Gaurav's success in his CA exams and career achievements were the direct result of his intense focus and dedication. His story demonstrates that even those who don't start at the top can achieve great things through **focused effort**.

2. **Act Fast and Learn Along the Way** – Gaurav's decision to leave his corporate job at 42 to start a business is a prime example of how taking **rapid action**, even in uncertain situations, can lead to success. His willingness to move quickly and adapt along the way helped him build a thriving business.

3. **Massive Action Yields Massive Results** – Gaurav didn't just start a business—he scaled it by taking **bold, massive action**. From building a team to landing significant clients, his ability to think big and act decisively helped him achieve substantial growth in a highly competitive market.

4. **Take Calculated Risks** – Gaurav's journey was marked by key risks, including leaving a stable job and investing in a new venture. His ability to take **calculated risks**, combined with rapid decision-making, helped him turn those risks into opportunities for success.

Gaurav Jain's story shows that success is not a product of luck or brilliance—it's the result of **focused effort**, **rapid action**, and **massive, bold moves**. His journey from corporate executive to successful entrepreneur proves that when you **act quickly, take calculated risks**, and **commit fully** to your goals, there's no limit to what you can achieve.

Story 6: Bhavik Vasa – A Journey of Curiosity, Resilience, and Bold Innovation

Bhavik Vasa's journey is a masterclass in how **curiosity, resilience, and bold action** can lead to transformative success. From his early lessons in negotiation to building a trailblazing fintech business, Bhavik's story demonstrates the power of **Focused, Rapid, and Massive Action (FRMA)** in turning uncertainty into opportunity.

Early Lessons in Negotiation and Humility

Bhavik's entrepreneurial spark was ignited at a young age when he learned a critical lesson from his father: **"You don't get what you deserve, you get what you negotiate."** This profound mantra became the foundation of his life, shaping how he approached every challenge.

Growing up in a family of small business owners, Bhavik learned quickly that the world owed him nothing. Success would come from his ability to **navigate challenges and negotiate through life.** These early lessons of humility and perseverance stayed with him through countless setbacks, shaping the resilient mindset that would fuel his future successes.

Key Advice from Bhavik:

- "The world won't hand you success—you have to negotiate for it. **Know your worth** and fight for what you deserve."

Focused Action: Setting Small, Achievable Targets

One of Bhavik's core success strategies is his ability to **focus on small, tangible goals** while keeping an eye on the bigger picture. After experiencing a setback in his academic life in India, Bhavik made a bold decision: he left for the U.S. on a one-way ticket with a promise to himself that he wouldn't return until he could afford it.

While juggling three jobs and studying, Bhavik set a clear, short-term goal: **earn enough to buy a return ticket to India.** Although it took 14 arduous months, this period of intense focus instilled in him the **invaluable lesson of breaking down ambitious dreams into a series of smaller, actionable steps.** This approach became a driving force in his life, helping him build one success after another.

Key Advice from Bhavik:

- "Big dreams are built on **small wins**. Set achievable targets, focus on them, and success will follow."

Rapid Action: Adapting to Change Without Hesitation

Bhavik's fintech career is a testament to his ability to **move quickly and adapt to emerging trends**. Entering the fintech space before it even had a name, Bhavik was an early adopter of digital payments and mobile technology while others were still focused on outdated systems like Blackberry and Palm.

His most defining moment came in 2009 when he made the bold decision to leave a thriving career in Silicon Valley to return to India. At that time, the Indian startup ecosystem was still in its infancy, with few investors and even fewer resources. But Bhavik saw **untapped potential**. By moving fast and **embracing uncertainty**, Bhavik positioned himself at the forefront of India's fintech revolution, playing a pivotal role in its growth.

Key Advice from Bhavik:

- "Don't wait for the perfect moment to act. The right time is **now**—move fast and **adapt along the way**."

Massive Action: Solving Real Problems with Purpose

Bhavik's most significant leap came with the launch of **GetVantage**, a fintech venture that disrupted India's traditional capital-raising systems. After a successful exit from his previous company, Bhavik saw a major gap in how traditional banks misunderstood digital businesses, demanding collateral for loans and stifling entrepreneurs.

GetVantage was Bhavik's bold answer to this problem. By offering frictionless access to growth capital through an **embedded finance platform**, Bhavik tackled the structural barriers that held back India's entrepreneurs. He didn't just create a company—he challenged the **status quo**, focusing on building a sustainable and scalable business. His massive action didn't stop at a vision; it involved navigating regulatory hurdles, building a robust tech stack, and ensuring full compliance—all while pushing the boundaries of fintech innovation.

Key Advice from Bhavik:

- "Massive problems require **massive action**. If you're not solving a real problem, you're not building something that lasts."

Key Lessons from Bhavik Vasa's Journey

1. **Negotiate and Navigate** – Bhavik's early lesson was clear: success is not a matter of entitlement; it arises from one's ability to navigate challenges and negotiate favorable outcomes throughout life's obstacles.

2. **Small Goals Lead to Big Wins** – Bhavik's journey underscores the power of setting **small, achievable goals** that build momentum. Whether it was saving for a return ticket or building a fintech empire, breaking down big dreams into manageable steps fueled his success.

3. **Embrace Discomfort** – Bhavik's philosophy is simple: **true magic happens outside your comfort zone.** From dismantling a VCR as a child to disrupting the fintech industry, his willingness to embrace discomfort has driven his biggest breakthroughs.

4. **Take Massive, Purpose-Driven Action** – Bhavik's decision to return to India and address critical challenges within the fintech space by founding GetVantage serves as a powerful testament to the **transformative power of impactful,**

purpose-driven action. His bold moves turned an industry on its head and empowered countless entrepreneurs.

Bhavik Vasa's journey is a testament to how **focused goals, rapid adaptation, and massive action** can turn challenges into opportunities. His willingness to negotiate for what he deserves, move fast when others hesitate, and take massive action to solve real-world problems has transformed the fintech landscape.

Story 7: Madhusudanan R. – From Vision to Victory: Building a Fintech Ecosystem

Madhusudanan R.'s journey is a powerful testament to how **Focused, Rapid, and Massive Action (FRMA)** can transform a fledgling idea into a thriving, impactful business. Starting in the early days of India's fintech revolution, Madhu's bold decisions, relentless focus, and ability to seize opportunities laid the foundation for a fintech ecosystem that has revolutionized the financial services landscape.

Early Days: Finding Purpose in a Shifting Landscape

In 2012-2013, Madhu, as he is often called, began his career at Visa, During this time he witnessed firsthand the inefficiencies in the banking sector. Despite their best intentions, **banks struggled to innovate** due to structural constraints. This lack of agility, combined with the emerging need for external partnerships, sparked an idea in Madhu: **build a platform** that would bridge the gap between financial institutions and innovators.

He saw how traditional banks struggled to partner with startups and how tech companies lacked the robust ecosystem to scale fintech solutions. This insight became the foundation of his vision—to create a platform that would **enable financial innovation at scale.**

Key Advice from Madhu:

- "Opportunities are everywhere, but only those who recognize them early and take action can turn them into gold."

Focused Action: Creating a Platform for Growth

Madhu's success was built on a **singular focus**: building an ecosystem that fostered fintech innovation. In the early years, he and his team worked tirelessly to solve the industry's "cold start" problem—how to get **banks and startups to collaborate** and create meaningful financial products.

Their focus on building **strong partnerships** was key. Instead of chasing every opportunity, Madhu concentrated on creating a platform that banks and startups alike could trust to scale their fintech solutions. This focused approach became their core strategy, allowing the company to slowly but steadily grow into a powerful player in the fintech space.

A pivotal moment came when Madhu and his team realized they needed to **say no to good opportunities** to focus on the great ones. They chose to concentrate on enabling fintech innovation on the issuing side, rather than spreading themselves too thin with other ventures like merchant payments. This laser focus helped them refine their platform and scale effectively.

Key Advice from Madhu:

- "You need to say **'no' to many good opportunities** to stay focused on the one great one that will change the game."

Rapid Action: Seizing Opportunities in Emerging Markets

Madhu's ability to act quickly on emerging trends was critical to his success. One of his boldest moves came during the rapid rise of UPI (Unified Payments Interface) in India. As UPI grew, banks began experiencing frequent downtime due to scalability issues. **Recognizing this as a massive opportunity**, Madhu quickly pivoted his company's focus to building solutions that could support banks in managing these challenges.

This move positioned his company as a key enabler in India's fintech ecosystem, allowing them to capture a significant portion of the market. Acting swiftly allowed Madhu to seize an opportunity that could have been easily missed by competitors waiting for perfect conditions.

His rapid decision-making extended internationally as well. When they entered Indonesia, they faced significant **regulatory challenges**. Instead of retreating, Madhu persisted, adapting the company's offerings to local regulations. After two years of effort, they finally gained traction, solidifying their presence in international markets.

Key Advice from Madhu:

- "In business, **speed is your best friend**. When opportunity knocks, answer immediately, or someone else will."

Massive Action: Scaling Through Acquisitions

Madhu's journey took a significant leap forward through **bold acquisitions**. By 2020, the company recognized a massive opportunity to provide core technology solutions to banks struggling to scale with the surge in demand for digital services. To capitalize on this, Madhu led a series of acquisitions in 2021-2022, bringing in companies with **complementary technologies**.

These acquisitions allowed the company to **scale rapidly**, expand its customer base, and strengthen its platform's capabilities. Integrating the new companies was no easy feat—there were misaligned expectations and operational challenges—but Madhu's commitment to his vision ensured that these acquisitions paid off, positioning his company as a leader in fintech infrastructure.

Key Advice from Madhu:

- "If you want to play big, you need to **act big**. Taking bold, massive steps is the only way to create real impact."

Key Lessons from Madhusudanan R.'s Journey

1. **Solving Big Problems Requires Focus** – Madhu's success was built on his **sharp focus** on solving a critical problem in fintech: enabling financial innovation through technology. This focus allowed his company to grow and thrive in a competitive space.

2. **Act Quickly on Emerging Trends** – Madhu's rapid pivot to solve UPI scalability issues is a perfect example of the importance of **acting swiftly** when opportunities arise. His quick action gave his company a competitive edge in a fast-growing market.

3. **Take Massive, Strategic Action** – The decision to **grow through acquisitions** was a bold move that helped Madhu scale his company and solidify its position as a fintech leader. By taking strategic, massive action, he was able to significantly expand his company's impact.

4. **Persistence Pays Off** – Madhu's entry into international markets like Indonesia shows the power of persistence. **Adaptation and resilience** allowed him to succeed, even when the initial path was filled with challenges.

Madhusudanan R.'s journey from a visionary fintech entrepreneur to a market leader showcases how **focused effort, rapid action, and bold moves** can turn a transformative idea into a reality. His ability to see emerging trends, act quickly, and take massive action made him a driving force behind a successful fintech ecosystem.

Story 8: Deepika Narayan Bhardwaj – Fearlessness and Persistence in the Face of Adversity

Deepika Narayan Bhardwaj's journey is a shining example of how **unwavering focus, fearlessness,** and **relentless persistence** can overcome even the most formidable challenges. From her shift from a software engineer to a TV journalist and then an activist championing men's rights in India, Deepika's story embodies the transformative power of **Focused, Rapid, and Massive Action (FRMA)**. Her fearless pursuit of justice in the face of criticism and societal opposition proves that **success is not about immediate rewards**, but about the relentless pursuit of a cause, no matter how daunting the journey.

Early Days: Finding Purpose in a Personal Crisis

Deepika's upbringing in Haryana instilled in her a sense of **independence** and **fearlessness**. Raised in a family that treated her and her brother equally, she was encouraged to chase her dreams. After completing her B. Tech in IT, Deepika landed a job at Infosys, a prestigious start to her career. But soon, she realized that **technology wasn't her calling**. She yearned for something more meaningful.

In 2008, **Deepika made a bold decision** to leave her stable, well-paying job and dive into TV journalism, despite having no background in the field. This leap into the unknown was driven by her deep desire for **personal fulfilment over financial security**. This first major life shift set the tone for the rest of her journey—choosing purpose over comfort, regardless of the risks.

Key Advice from Deepika:

- "It's never too late to walk away from a life that doesn't fulfill you. **Follow your heart, even if it's risky.**"

Focused Action: A New Path in Activism

Deepika's life took a dramatic turn in 2011 when her family faced a false dowry and domestic violence accusation. This personal crisis opened her eyes to the **misuse of laws** meant to protect women, prompting her to research men who had suffered similar fates. This painful experience ignited her passion to raise awareness and advocate for men's rights, and **her focus shifted entirely** toward this cause.

Her breakthrough project, the **documentary "Martyrs of Marriage,"** was born from this focus. Taking on the challenge of producing a documentary, she took a sabbatical from her job, pouring herself into the project. Despite societal opposition and facing personal attacks, **Deepika's focus on exposing the truth never wavered**. Her documentary, released on Netflix, sparked international discussions and placed a spotlight on an often-overlooked issue. **Deepika's unwavering focus on her mission** allowed her to create a significant impact despite all odds.

Key Advice from Deepika:

- "If you believe in something, let nothing distract you from your mission. **Stay true to your purpose**, no matter how tough it gets."

Rapid Action: Making Timely Decisions

While Deepika's journey is characterized by unwavering persistence, her ability to make **swift, decisive decisions** when necessary has proven instrumental to her progress. When she realized that balancing her job with producing "Martyrs of Marriage" was impossible, **Deepika quickly requested a one-year sabbatical**. This decision enabled her to dedicate her full attention and energy to the project, ultimately ensuring its success.

Her next swift move came after the success of "Martyrs of Marriage" when she launched her second documentary, "India's Sons." **Despite financial challenges, Deepika acted quickly** to secure funding and begin production. Her capacity to act decisively in key moments has propelled her activism forward, overcoming the obstacles that often paralyze others.

Key Advice from Deepika:

- "There's never a perfect time to act, but **hesitation only holds you back**. Leap when you know it's right."

Massive Action: Bold Moves in an Unforgiving Environment

Deepika's decision to **fight for men's rights in India**, a nation where women's rights dominate public discourse, was a bold and courageous step. She faced **intense criticism and personal risks**, especially with her daring decision to expose cases where women had filed **false accusations**. One such case in 2021, where a woman filed nine false rape charges against different men, became a national sensation when Deepika **boldly revealed the woman's identity**.

In 2023, Deepika took her advocacy to the next level by founding the **Incom Now Foundation**, an NGO dedicated to men's rights and providing legal aid to those falsely accused. This marked a significant shift from individual activism to creating a **sustainable framework for long-term change. Deepika's massive actions**, despite the societal backlash, cemented her role as a fearless activist and changemaker.

Key Advice from Deepika:

- "You can't make change without shaking things up. **Don't be afraid to take massive, bold steps** for what you believe in."

Lessons from Deepika Narayan Bhardwaj's Journey

1. **Fearlessness is Key to Overcoming Adversity** – Her entire journey reflects her **fearlessness**. From leaving a stable career to tackling controversial societal issues, her courage

to face challenges head-on has been the foundation of her success.

2. **Persistence Over Immediate Results** – Deepika's story is a powerful reminder that **persistence is key**. From producing documentaries to fighting legal battles, her long-term dedication to her cause has helped her overcome setbacks and gain traction, even when success wasn't immediate.

3. **Taking Bold, Massive Action** – Deepika's journey shows that true change requires **bold, massive actions**. Her willingness to take personal and legal risks to expose systemic flaws in society has made her a leader in the fight for justice.

4. **The Importance of Timely Decisions** – Though her work spans years, her ability to make quick, effective decisions at crucial moments—like requesting a sabbatical or securing funding for her projects—has been essential to her success.

Deepika Narayan Bhardwaj's journey is a story of resilience, fearless pursuit, and relentless commitment to justice. Her ability to focus on a cause, act quickly, and take bold, massive steps proves that **transformative change is possible** for those who dare to confront adversity head-on.

Story 9: Sandeep Mall – A Journey of Resilience, Transformation, and Reinvention

Sandeep Mall's story is a powerful narrative of **resilience, self-reflection**, and the transformative power of **Focused, Rapid, and Massive Action (FRMA)** to overcome life's toughest challenges and reinvent oneself completely. From navigating severe financial setbacks in business to turning his health around after a life-threatening injury, Sandeep's journey is a testament to the power of **determination, strategic thinking**, and **unwavering courage** in creating a meaningful life.

Early Struggles: Navigating Financial Setbacks

Sandeep's journey began in the small town of Purulia, West Bengal, where he was deeply influenced by his Marwari family's entrepreneurial values. It was almost a given that he would enter business rather than pursue a traditional job. Yet, his early ventures were fraught with **obstacles and setbacks.**

His first business—digitizing accounting records—failed due to the market's resistance to embracing technology at the time. His equipment crashed multiple times, eventually forcing him to shut down operations. But **instead of giving up**, Sandeep used these failures as stepping stones to build resilience and adaptability.

Another major setback occurred when the client for his Faridabad factory went bankrupt after two years, leaving his venture hanging by a thread. Despite the dire circumstances, Sandeep adhered to his principle of **not taking personal money out of the family business.** This discipline and **commitment to financial prudence** helped him navigate through these challenging times.

Advice from Sandeep:

- "Resilience is your greatest asset. **No matter how tough things get, never stop moving forward.**"

Focused Action: Building a Thriving Export-Oriented Company

One of Sandeep's core strengths has been his ability to **focus on long-term goals**, even when confronted with immediate challenges. When his initial client went under, Sandeep quickly regrouped and pivoted his company's strategy to focus on **export markets**, thereby transforming a struggling factory into a successful, export-driven business.

Today, **95% of his company's revenue comes from exports,** a remarkable turnaround built on his relentless focus on global growth and sustainability. This shift didn't happen overnight; it required years of **strategic focus, networking, and calculated risks.**

Through persistence, Sandeep was able to build a robust business that could withstand external shocks.

Advice from Sandeep:

- "Focus on **building a strong foundation** before aiming for the sky. **Short-term sacrifices lead to long-term success.**"

Rapid Action: Pivoting During Crisis

In 2008, the U.S. recession hit Sandeep's business hard. With most of his clients based in the U.S., sales plummeted, pushing his company to the brink of collapse. At this critical juncture, **Sandeep didn't hesitate**—he made the tough decision to **shut down his largest U.S. client**, despite the immediate financial hit.

But instead of waiting for things to get better, Sandeep quickly pivoted to explore new markets, including Australia. **Within months, he secured a major project in the Australian mining sector**, which not only stabilized his company but also **diversified his business across geographies**. This bold move to enter a new market during a downturn was a game-changer, proving that **quick, decisive action** can turn crises into opportunities.

Advice from Sandeep:

- "In business, **timing is everything**. Don't hesitate when the moment calls for quick, decisive action."

Massive Action: Reinventing His Health and Life

Sandeep's most profound transformation came not in business, but in his **health**. In 2008, he was involved in a severe car accident, suffering a neck injury that required **spinal surgery**. This incident became a **wake-up call**. Sandeep realized that years of focusing solely on work had **left his health in a disastrous state**—he was overweight, unfit, and on the brink of severe health complications.

Faced with this reality, Sandeep **took massive action**. He overhauled his lifestyle, embracing a strict regimen of exercise, a healthier diet, and a commitment to **prioritizing his health**. Within a few years, he underwent a dramatic transformation, shedding the extra weight and returning to fitness. This journey was about more than just physical fitness—it led Sandeep to embark on a **deeper journey of self-reflection** and emotional well-being. He sought counseling, learned to manage his stress, and even embraced hobbies like **wildlife photography**, which helped him find **inner peace and balance**.

Today, Sandeep is not just **physically fit**—he's **mentally stronger** and **emotionally more centered**, a living example of how massive action can reinvent not just a career, but an entire life.

Advice from Sandeep:

- "Success isn't just about work. **Take care of your body, mind, and spirit**, or you'll burn out before you achieve your dreams."

Lessons from Sandeep Mall's Journey

1. **Resilience in the Face of Adversity** – Sandeep's journey is a **masterclass in resilience**. His ability to navigate through **financial setbacks**, adapt to changing markets, and rebuild his business from the ground up shows that persistence can overcome any obstacle.

2. **Focus on Long-Term Sustainability** – Sandeep's decision to **live within his means**, even during tough times, helped him build a **sustainable business**. His focus on **long-term success**, rather than quick wins, was key to his growth.

3. **Act Quickly and Decisively** – When faced with the 2008 recession, Sandeep made the **tough decision** to shut down his largest client and explore new markets. His **rapid actions** allowed him to save his business and thrive in international markets.

4. **Massive Personal Transformation** – Sandeep's journey from **neglecting his health** to becoming **physically fit** and **emotionally balanced** is a powerful example of how **massive action can lead to complete reinvention.** His transformation shows that it's **never too late** to make big changes in life.

Sandeep Mall's journey is a **powerful reminder** that true success isn't just about professional achievements—it's about building a life that aligns with your **values, health,** and **personal fulfilment.** His story demonstrates that with resilience, focus, and massive action, you can not only overcome life's toughest challenges but also **reinvent yourself completely.**

Story 10: Nilesh Karandikar – Building a Vision from Scratch through Focus, Resilience, and Innovation

Nilesh Karandikar's entrepreneurial journey exemplifies the transformative power of **Focused, Rapid, and Massive Action (FRMA).** From his humble beginnings in Pune to becoming a pioneer in the manufacturing industry, Nilesh has overcome numerous challenges to establish a thriving company in a niche market. His story is one of **relentless focus, bold decision-making, and the resilience** needed to succeed against the odds.

Early Beginnings: Learning from the Ground Up

Nilesh grew up in Pune, where his passion for engineering was inspired by his father, who introduced **laser-cutting technology** to India in 1986. This early exposure to innovation set the stage for Nilesh's future ambitions. His journey took off when he pursued mechanical engineering at the **Government College of Engineering Pune,** where he gained hands-on experience at Tata Motors through a sandwich course. This deepened his interest in building something of his own.

From the beginning, Nilesh's vision was clear: he didn't just want a career, he wanted to **create an enterprise** that blended his technical expertise with the dream of offering innovative industrial solutions. Early on, a challenge from his boss at Tata Motors pushed him to innovate, emphasizing that India had great engineers but relied too heavily on imported equipment. This sparked his determination to dive into the field of **industrial manipulators**, a relatively unexplored area in India.

Advice from Nilesh:

- "When you have a passion, nurture it and **let it guide your decisions**, even when others don't see the potential."

Focused Action: Carving a Niche through Determination

Nilesh's career has been defined by his **sharp focus** on building something unique in a specific niche—industrial manipulators for assembly lines. Instead of taking lucrative job offers abroad, including one from a renowned company in Germany, Nilesh chose to return to India in 2003 to **pursue his vision**.

Initially, he partnered with a German company to sell industrial equipment in India. However, it quickly became clear that the high cost of imported machinery was unsustainable for the Indian market. Rather than giving up, Nilesh pivoted and focused on manufacturing these machines **locally**, offering more affordable, high-quality solutions tailored to Indian companies. This **laser-focused approach** to solving a specific market need became the bedrock of his business success.

Advice from Nilesh:

- "Success doesn't come from doing everything; it comes from **doing one thing exceptionally well**. Focus is the key."

Rapid Action: Making Decisive Moves in Critical Moments

Nilesh's ability to take **swift, decisive action** has been a hallmark of his success. A defining moment came early in his company's journey when a **critical issue** arose with the machines installed at Tata Motors. A crack developed in a key component that could have led to a disaster. Nilesh took immediate action, dismantling the machines overnight and replacing the faulty parts. This **rapid response** not only saved the client's project but also earned their **long-term trust**, laying the foundation for repeat business.

Another instance of Nilesh's exceptional decision-making capabilities emerged when the COVID-19 pandemic-induced lockdowns significantly disrupted his production timelines, necessitating the construction of new assembly facilities. Once the lockdown was lifted, Nilesh acted fast, completing the construction of a state-of-the-art assembly facility within a year. This decision enabled him to take on major projects from **automotive giants** like Daimler, Maruti Suzuki, Mahindra & Mahindra, and Tata Motors, boosting his company's growth.

Advice from Nilesh:

- "When faced with a crisis, **don't wait** for it to resolve itself. Take immediate action to prevent bigger issues down the road."

Massive Action: Scaling and Innovating Despite the Odds

Throughout his career, Nilesh has embraced **massive action**, often in the face of significant risks. One of his boldest moves was accepting **challenging projects** for equipment his company had never built before. With no prior experience in certain types of machinery, Nilesh took on these orders and worked relentlessly to develop innovative solutions from scratch. His philosophy of **"jumping into the water to learn to swim"** paid off, leading to successful project deliveries and establishing strong client relationships.

Nilesh didn't stop at technical challenges—he took **massive steps** in expanding his company's infrastructure, acquiring new clients, and increasing production capacity. These bold actions enabled his company to **double its turnover** in the years following the pandemic, a clear testament to his **visionary thinking** and ability to take calculated risks.

Advice from Nilesh:

- "Big rewards come from big risks. **Don't hesitate** to take massive action when you see the opportunity."

Lessons from Nilesh Karandikar's Journey

1. **Stay Focused on Your Vision** – Nilesh's success is rooted in his **unwavering focus** on a niche market. By committing to building industrial manipulators, he established a strong reputation and became a leader in the industry.

2. **Act Quickly in Critical Moments** – Nilesh's ability to make **rapid decisions,** such as fixing faulty machines overnight or building new facilities quickly after the pandemic, earned him **client trust** and played a crucial role in his company's success.

3. **Take Massive Action Despite the Risks** – Nilesh's decision to accept **challenging projects** and develop new types of machinery, even without prior experience, highlights the importance of **massive action**. His bold approach allowed him to grow his business and build lasting relationships with major clients.

4. **Believe in Long-Term Potential** – Nilesh's **confidence in India's industrial growth**, even when others doubted the market's potential, gave him the conviction to build his business locally. His foresight and belief in the country's progress enabled him to create a **thriving enterprise.**

Nilesh Karandikar's remarkable journey serves as an inspiring example of the transformative power of **focused vision, rapid**

action, and massive steps. His journey is a powerful reminder that **success comes from commitment, resilience, and the willingness to take bold risks**—even when the path forward seems uncertain.

FRMA MANTRA FOR A STUDENT

Students, you are at the start of an amazing journey, but dreaming alone is not enough. You require action —not merely any action but **focused, rapid, massive action.** This is your weapon to achieve big, to stand out, and to create your future.

What does FRMA mean for you?

Focused action: Get your priorities straight

Too many distractions? Too many ideas? Stop. Focus. What matters?

Here's how you do it:

- Define one clear goal. What's your next big thing? Cracking an exam, learning a skill, or building a network?

- Break it down into small milestones and tackle them one at a time.

- Ditch distractions. Use techniques like Pomodoro to stay laser-focused.

Example: Ritesh Agarwal, the founder of OYO Rooms, started as a student. His focus? Learn the startup game. He attended conferences, studied successful entrepreneurs, and found his niche in the hospitality sector.

Quote:

> *"Success is no accident. It is hard work, perseverance, learning, studying, sacrifice, and most of all, love of what you are doing or learning to do."*

> **– Narayana Murthy**

Quote:

> *"Your dreams are valid, but only hard work turns them into reality."*

> **– Meghana Srivastava, CBSE Class 12 All-India Topper**

Rapid action: Start now, not tomorrow

Stop waiting for the perfect time. It doesn't exist. Rapid action is about taking the first step immediately.

Here's how you do it:

- Apply for that internship or competition today.
- Reach out to a mentor or professor right now.
- Start that project or side hustle you've been thinking about.

Example: Ananya Gupta, an engineering student, dreamed of a tech startup. She didn't wait for graduation. She started small, built projects, and today runs a recognized AI-based learning tool.

Quote:

"It's not about ideas. It's about making ideas happen."

– Nandan Nilekani

Quote:

"I never gave up. I believed in myself, and I pushed through every challenge."

– R Praggnanandhaa, Chess Grandmaster

Massive action: Be bold, Think big

Success doesn't come from playing small. Massive action means stepping out of your comfort zone.

Here's how you do it:

- Participate in national competitions or hackathons.
- Apply for global scholarships or exchange programs.
- Network like your life depends on it—even as a student.

Example: Shruti Sharma, a small-town student, applied for the prestigious Chevening Scholarship. Her massive action paid off, taking her to the UK and a career as an international policy advisor.

Quote:

– Ratan Tata

Quote:

"The key to success is consistency and courage to dream big."

— **Hima Das, Indian Athlete and World Junior Champion**

Challenges? FRMA solves them

1. "I don't know what to focus on."

Answer: Explore. Try internships, join clubs, and take short courses. Find what excites you.

2. "I'm too busy with classes."

Answer: Prioritize. Block 1-2 hours daily for personal growth outside academics.

3. "What if I fail?"

Answer: Failing is learning. The faster you fail, the faster you succeed.

How to implement FRMA

Step 1: Write your goal.

Be specific. Example: "Learn Python and get an internship in 6 months."

Step 2: Create a focus blueprint.

Divide your goal into weekly milestones:

- Week 1: Research companies.
- Week 2: Learn Python basics.
- Week 3: Build a mini project.

Step 3: Take rapid action.

Start today. Sign up for a course or contact a mentor.

Step 4: Commit to massive action.

Participate in a hackathon or publish your work online.

Practical exercises

1. Time audit

Track your activities for a week. Eliminate time-wasters and replace them with growth actions.

2. The 30-day challenge

Pick one goal. Take one action daily for 30 days. Example: Solve one coding problem every day.

3. Networking goal

Connect with 5 people in your field this month. Start conversations, ask questions, learn.

Wrap-up: Your future is in your hands

You have time, energy, and the power to create your future. Embrace the FRMA mantra – **Focus, Rapid Action, and Massive Action** – as your guiding principle. The journey won't be easy, but greatness is always earned.

Quote to remember:

> *"The best way to predict the future is to create it."*

> – **Abraham Lincoln**

Start your journey today. Don't wait. Greatness awaits you.

FRMA MANTRA FOR A FRESH JOB SEEKER

Stepping into the job market can feel overwhelming, but it's also a world of opportunity. The key is not to wait for luck but to create your own success. The **FRMA mantra—Focused, Rapid, Massive Action—is your blueprint** to land the job you want and kickstart your career with confidence.

What does FRMA mean for a fresh job seeker?

Focused action: Target the right opportunities

Instead of applying for every job opening that comes your way, meticulously research and identify roles that truly align with your skills, interests, and career aspirations.

Here's how you do it:

- Research industries and companies that excite you.
- Tailor your resume and cover letter for each application.
- Prioritize quality over quantity in your job applications.

Example: Ashwini Iyer, a mechanical engineering graduate, spent two weeks researching companies aligned with her interests in renewable energy. By tailoring her applications and networking directly with recruiters, she secured a role at a top solar energy firm.

Quote:

"Identify your strengths and align them with your goals. Then, focus all your energy on chasing those opportunities."

— **Rajat Sharma, IIM Bangalore Topper**

Rapid action: Don't wait, start applying

The biggest mistake job seekers make is delaying. Rapid action is about taking consistent steps daily, no matter how small.

Here's how you do it:

- Set a target to apply to 3-5 well-researched jobs every day.
- Reach out to professionals on LinkedIn for advice and referrals.
- Attend job fairs and webinars to expand your network.

Example: Rohan Verma, a computer science graduate, applied to 50 companies in two weeks and followed up with personalized emails. His persistence landed him a role in a fast-growing tech startup.

Quote:

*"Take small steps, but take them every day.
Momentum builds success."*

— **Ananya Singh, 2021 Campus Placement Topper**

Massive action: Go beyond the basics

Standing out in a competitive job market requires bold moves. Massive action is about doing what others won't.

Here's how you do it:

- Create a personal portfolio or project that showcases your skills.
- Reach out directly to hiring managers with a value proposition.
- Volunteer, intern, or freelance in your desired industry to gain relevant experience.

Example: Priya Menon, a literature graduate, couldn't find her dream job in publishing. She launched a blog analyzing literary trends and shared it on LinkedIn. Her blog caught the attention of a leading publishing house, earning her an interview and the job.

Quote:

"The boldest actions often lead to the biggest breakthroughs."

— **Niharika Sharma, Founder of Career Catalyst**

Challenges? FRMA solves them

1. "I don't have enough experience."

Answer: Focus on your transferable skills. Highlight projects, internships, or volunteer work that demonstrate your capabilities.

2. "I'm not getting interview calls."

Answer: Refine your resume and LinkedIn profile. Use Rapid Action to follow up with recruiters after applying.

3. "The competition is too tough."

Answer: Take Massive Action to stand out. Create a video introduction, build a portfolio, or take an online certification to boost your profile.

How to implement FRMA

Step 1: Write your job target.

Be specific. Example: "Secure a marketing role at a leading FMCG company within 3 months."

Step 2: Create a focus blueprint.

- Week 1: Research companies and update your resume.
- Week 2: Apply to at least 15 targeted roles and network on LinkedIn.
- Week 3: Prepare for interviews by practicing common questions.

Step 3: Take rapid action.

Set daily application goals and stick to them. Reach out to at least one professional or mentor each day.

Step 4: Commit to massive action.

Showcase your initiative by building a portfolio, volunteering, or creating content relevant to your field.

Practical exercises

1. The 10-10-10 rule

Each week, aim to:

* Apply to 10 jobs.

* Connect with 10 professionals in your field.

* Follow up on 10 applications or conversations.

2. Build your personal pitch

Craft a 60-second elevator pitch highlighting your skills, achievements, and goals. Practice delivering it confidently.

3. Showcase your work

Start a blog, create a GitHub portfolio, or share LinkedIn posts demonstrating your expertise.

Wrap-up: Your career begins today

The job market rewards those who are proactive, persistent, and bold. By consistently applying the FRMA mantra – **Focus, Rapid Action, and Massive Action** – you can navigate this challenging terrain with unwavering clarity and unwavering confidence. Remember, the difference between ordinary and extraordinary is decisive action.

Quote to remember:

"Dreams don't work unless you do."

– **APJ Abdul Kalam**

Start now. Your dream job is waiting for you.

FRMA MANTRA FOR A MID-AGED EMPLOYEE OR ENTREPRENEUR

You're in your 30s or 40s, balancing work, family, and aspirations. At this stage, it's easy to feel stuck in routine or hesitate to take risks. However, this period also presents a unique opportunity for profound personal and professional growth – a golden era to redefine success on your terms and truly push the boundaries of your potential. The FRMA mantra—focused, rapid, massive action— is the game-changer you need to elevate your career or business to the next level.

What does FRMA mean for you as a mid-aged professional or entrepreneur?

Focused action: Sharpen your priorities

You've been in the game long enough to know your strengths. Now is the time to channel them into a focused vision.

Here's how you do it:

- Identify what truly matters—whether it's climbing the career ladder, scaling your business, or creating a personal brand.

- Audit your time and energy. Eliminate what doesn't contribute to your goals.

- Set a clear roadmap with measurable milestones.

Example: Rajesh Sinha, a mid-level manager in Mumbai, realized he was stuck on a plateau. He decided to focus on his leadership skills. Rajesh joined an executive program, took on challenging projects, and within two years, became the regional head of his company.

Quote:

> *"The secret of focus is saying no to good opportunities*
> *so you can say yes to the great ones."*

— **Nitin Kamath, Founder of Zerodha**

Rapid action: Time waits for no one

Experience gives you an edge, but in today's fast-paced world, speed is critical. Rapid action is about leveraging your expertise to act decisively.

Here's how you do it:

- Don't overthink. Once you've identified an opportunity, act on it immediately.

- Take quick steps to learn new tools or skills relevant to your field.

- Cut down on time-consuming processes. Streamline and delegate.

Example: Neha Gupta, a mid-aged entrepreneur, pivoted her traditional retail business to an e-commerce model during the pandemic. She took swift action to learn digital marketing and implement changes within weeks, saving her business and increasing revenue.

Quote:

> *"Speed is your weapon. In a world that waits for no one,*
> *acting fast gives you the upper hand."*

– **Vineeta Singh, CEO of Sugar Cosmetics**

Massive action: Go bold, think big

At this stage, small moves won't create big changes. Massive action is about being bold enough to challenge the status quo.

Here's how you do it:

- Take on a high-stakes project that pushes your limits.

- Expand your network. Connect with mentors, industry leaders, and peers.

- Make bold decisions—whether it's switching careers, entering a new market, or launching an ambitious product.

Example: Amit Bhatt, a 42-year-old entrepreneur, decided to enter the international market despite skepticism from his peers. His massive action led to a breakthrough deal in Dubai, doubling his business revenue in just one year.

Quote:

"Big results require big moves. Don't be afraid to go all in."

– Byju Raveendran, Founder of BYJU'S

Challenges? FRMA has the solutions

1. "I don't have time."

Answer: You don't need more time; you need to prioritize. Block out distractions and delegate.

2. "I'm afraid to take risks."

Answer: The only true risk is staying stagnant. Start with small calculated steps and build momentum.

3. "What if I fail?"

Answer: Failure is a stepping stone. Learn, adapt, and keep moving forward.

How to implement FRMA

Step 1: Define your focus.

- Be specific. Example: "Increase business revenue by 50% within the next 12 months."

Step 2: Take rapid action.

- Start today. Enroll in a course, hire a mentor, or apply for a stretch role.

Step 3: Commit to massive action.

- Launch a bold initiative, such as a product revamp, business pivot, or public speaking engagement.

Practical exercises

1. Time audit

- Track your weekly activities. Identify and eliminate tasks that don't align with your goals.

2. Skill upgrade plan

- List three critical skills for your next role or venture. Dedicate one hour daily to mastering them.

3. Massive action challenge

- Identify one bold action you've been postponing. Commit to completing it within the next month.

Real-life inspiration

Kavita Mehta: From Employee to Entrepreneur

At 39, Kavita quit her corporate job to start a sustainable fashion brand. She focused on her niche, acted rapidly to build her network, and took massive action by participating in global trade fairs. Today, her brand is a market leader in eco-friendly apparel.

Quote:

> *"Age is just a number. What matters is how willing you are to adapt, learn, and act."*

> **– Kavita Mehta**

Anil Deshmukh: The Bold Career Switch

Anil, a middle-aged IT professional, decided to switch to a career in data science. He focused on acquiring the necessary skills through rapid upskilling and took massive action by creating a portfolio of projects. His efforts landed him a senior data science role at a multinational firm.

Quote:

> *"Success is not about starting young; it's about starting strong."*

– **Anil Deshmukh**

Wrap-up: Your best years are now

This is your moment to shine. **The unique blend of** experience, skills, and network you've built are powerful assets. Combine them with the FRMA mantra to elevate your career or business. **Focus, act swiftly, and take bold steps.** It's never too late to achieve greatness.

Quote to remember:

> *"It's not about how old you are; it's about how bold you are."*

– **Dr. Kiran Mazumdar-Shaw, Founder of Biocon**

Your next breakthrough awaits. Take that first step today!

FRMA MANTRA FOR BUSINESS LEADERS AND SUCCESSFUL ENTREPRENEURS

Taking Your Success to the Next Level

You've achieved significant milestones as a business leader or entrepreneur, but you know there's more to accomplish. Greatness doesn't stop at one peak—it drives you to climb higher, innovate further, and grow faster. The FRMA mantra—focused, rapid, massive action—is your key to unlocking your next level of success and dominating your industry.

What does FRMA mean for you as a business leader or entrepreneur?

Focused action: Master clarity amidst complexity

Running a business or leading an organization often means juggling multiple priorities. However, true progress hinges on **focused action**. This involves sharpening your vision and eliminating distractions that dilute your impact.

Here's how you do it:

- Define what's next: Is it scaling, diversifying, or innovating? Choose one goal that will create the biggest impact.

- Identify the resources, teams, and skills you need to achieve that goal.

- Ruthlessly eliminate low-priority tasks or ventures.

Example:

Narayana Murthy, co-founder of Infosys, emphasized clarity when building Infosys into a global IT giant. His focus on customer-centric innovation, quality, and team excellence helped him transform a small startup into an internationally renowned company.

Quote

"In God we trust; everybody else must bring data."

– Narayana Murthy

Rapid action: Speed is your competitive edge

In business, time is money. Delaying decisions or procrastinating can cost you opportunities. Rapid action ensures you stay ahead of the competition and sustain the momentum necessary for growth.

Here's how you do it:

- Implement a culture of swift decision-making and execution within your organization.
- Use rapid prototypes and experiments to test ideas before scaling them.
- Embrace technology and tools that improve efficiency and reduce time to market.

Example:

Anand Mahindra, Chairman of Mahindra Group, is known for quick and bold decisions. During the 2008 recession, Mahindra acquired Satyam Computers rapidly and turned it into a highly profitable IT services company, reinforcing Mahindra Group's global presence.

Quote:

"Speed is not just about moving fast;
it's about being the first to grab the opportunity."

– Anand Mahindra

Massive action: Go big or go home

Success demands bold moves. Massive action is about making decisions that transform industries, inspire teams, and create exponential growth.

Here's how you do it:

- Take calculated risks to enter new markets or introduce groundbreaking products.
- Invest in building an extraordinary team that shares your vision and ambition.
- Leverage your brand to create influence and partnerships.

Example: Ratan Tata took massive action when he introduced the Tata Nano—a car for the masses. Though the Nano didn't achieve sustained success, the bold move reshaped how the world viewed Indian manufacturing and innovation.

Quote:

"If you want to walk fast, walk alone.
But if you want to walk far, walk together."

– Ratan Tata

Challenges? FRMA has the solutions

1. "I don't know how to scale further."

Answer: Use the FRMA mantra to pinpoint high-growth opportunities, like international markets or new technology integrations.

2. "The competition is too intense."

Answer: Innovate rapidly. Stay ahead by testing, adapting, and iterating faster than your competitors.

3. "I'm afraid to take risks at this level."

Answer: Every big move carries risks, but calculated risks based on data and market research often pay off.

How to implement FRMA

Step 1: Define your focus.

- Decide on one transformative goal for the next 12 months. Example: "Double market share in North America."

Step 2: Take rapid action.

- Assign clear tasks and deadlines to your team to start executing immediately.

Step 3: Commit to massive action.

- Make a bold move, like launching a global campaign, acquiring a competitor, or entering a high-risk, high-reward market.

Practical exercises

1. Vision refinement tool

- Write your 5-year vision. Identify the single most impactful goal that aligns with your vision.

2. Rapid decision framework

- Create a checklist of criteria for quick decision-making (e.g., ROI, market potential, and team capability).

3. The bold move challenge

- Identify one bold action you've hesitated to take. Commit to executing it within the next 30 days.

Real-life inspiration

Vineeta Singh: Building Sugar Cosmetics into a Household Brand

Vineeta Singh, the founder of Sugar Cosmetics, took focused action to identify a gap in the Indian beauty market for bold yet affordable cosmetics. Her rapid product launches and massive marketing campaigns made Sugar a leader in a competitive market.

Quote:

"Don't wait for opportunities—create them."

– **Vineeta Singh**

Narayana Peesapaty: The Edible Cutlery Visionary

Narayana, founder of Bakey's, redefined sustainability with edible cutlery. His massive action of challenging plastic use globally put his company on the map, inspiring a global movement for eco-friendly alternatives.

Quote:

"Think big, start small, and move fast."

– **Narayana Peesapaty**

Wrap-up: The next level is yours to conquer

You've accomplished a great deal already, but greatness isn't about resting on your laurels—it's about striving for more. The **FRMA mantra** empowers you to focus on what matters, act swiftly to capitalize on opportunities, and take bold actions that redefine success.

Quote to remember:

"Success is a journey, not a destination. Keep pushing the boundaries."

– **Mukesh Ambani**

Your next chapter of growth awaits. Take the first step today—focused, rapid, massive action!

FRMA MANTRA FOR RETURNING MOTHERS AND HOUSEWIVES FROM HOME TO HUSTLE: REDEFINING YOUR FUTURE

Being a mother and a homemaker is one of the most demanding yet often unappreciated roles. If you aspire to start your own business or re-entering the corporate world, your journey begins with a decision—to take control of your ambitions. The FRMA mantra—focused, rapid, massive action—serves as a powerful blueprint to rediscover your potential and achieve your dreams.

What does FRMA mean for you as a housewife?

Focused action: Find clarity in your aspirations

The first step is deciding what you truly want. Is it a business that reflects your passions? Or a corporate career that leverages your skills? Focused action helps you gain clarity amidst all the options.

Here's how you do it:

- Write down your dreams—what excites you most about your next step?
- Assess your skills and interests to align them with your goal.
- Research opportunities in your chosen field or industry.

Example:

Ritu Bhagat, a homemaker for 12 years, wanted to support her family financially. She focused on her love for cooking and started a small home catering business. By concentrating on niche markets, she turned her passion into a profitable enterprise.

Quote:

"Clarity is the most powerful tool for turning dreams into reality."

– **Falguni Nayar, Founder of Nykaa**

Rapid action: Start now, not tomorrow

Once you've identified your goal, the next step is to take immediate action. Procrastination is the enemy of progress.

Here's how you do it:

- If you're eyeing entrepreneurship, create a simple business plan and start testing your idea.

- If you're looking for a corporate job, update your resume and LinkedIn profile today.

- Start small but act fast—enroll in a course, apply for jobs, or connect with industry professionals.

Example:

Shalini Mehta had been out of the workforce for 8 years. She quickly upskilled in digital marketing through online courses and started freelancing. Within a year, she landed a full-time job at a reputed marketing firm.

Quote:

"Speed is what sets achievers apart. Don't wait for the perfect moment—start with what you have."

– **Richa Kar, Founder of Zivame**

Massive action: Dream big, act boldly

Success lies beyond the boundaries of your comfort zone. Massive action requires bold decisions and consistent effort.

Here's how you do it:

- As an entrepreneur: Leverage social media to market your business aggressively.

- As a job seeker: Apply to roles that challenge you and reflect your potential.

- Build a strong support system—seek mentorship, network with like-minded individuals, and ask for help when needed.

Example:

Seema Verma, after years as a homemaker, launched a home décor business online. Her massive action included participating in trade expos, collaborating with influencers, and scaling her business nationwide.

Quote:

"Courage is like a muscle. The more you use it, the stronger it gets."

– Kiran Mazumdar-Shaw, Founder of Biocon

Challenges? FRMA has the solutions

1. **"I don't know where to start."**

   Answer: Start small. Begin with online research, part-time projects, or courses to test your ideas.

2. **"I feel out of touch."**

   Answer: Upskilling is easier than ever. Platforms like Coursera, Udemy, and LinkedIn Learning offer courses for all levels.

3. **"I'm afraid of failing."**

   Answer: Failure is just feedback. Use it to improve and move forward.

How to implement FRMA

Step 1: Define your focus.

- Set a specific goal: "Start a fashion boutique from home" or "Land a job in HR within 6 months."

Step 2: Take rapid action.

- Dedicate 2-3 hours daily to your goal. Update your skills, create a portfolio, or start networking.

Step 3: Commit to massive action.

- Showcase your work on social media or professional platforms. Take bold steps like pitching to investors or applying for leadership roles.

Practical exercises

1. **Goal clarity exercise**
   - Write down your top three goals. Break each into smaller, actionable steps.

2. **The networking challenge**
   - Reach out to 5 professionals or entrepreneurs in your field this month.

3. **The courage tracker**
   - Identify one bold action to take each week, whether it's pitching a business idea or attending an industry event.

Real-life inspiration

Neha Sharma: From Homemaker to Boutique Owner

Neha, a mother of two, always dreamed of running her own clothing business. With focused action, she researched suppliers and trends. Her rapid action involved using WhatsApp to sell to friends and family. Massive action came when she launched her brand on Instagram. Today, her boutique has customers across India.

Quote:

"Success starts with a decision to try. The effort you put in will always come back to you."

— **Neha Sharma**

Anita Tiwari: Back to Corporate Success

After a decade away from the workforce to raise her kids, Anita decided it was time to return to her career. She focused on brushing up her technical skills and attended webinars to stay updated. Her bold, massive action came when she attended a job fair, confidently showcasing her value to potential employers. She now works as a project manager in a leading IT firm.

Quote:

"Your comeback can be greater than your setback if you're willing to work for it."

— **Anita Tiwari**

Wrap-up: Your time is now

You've spent years giving your best to your family. Now, it's your turn to rediscover your ambitions and create a future you're proud of. The FRMA mantra will guide you—focus on what matters, act swiftly, and take bold steps to build the life you deserve.

The journey ahead is yours to shape. Start today with focused, rapid, massive action!

Quote to remember:

"It's never too late to be what you might have been."

— **George Eliot**

FRMA MANTRA FOR PERSONAL RELATIONSHIPS

Rekindling Connections, Rebuilding Bonds

Personal relationships are the foundation of a fulfilling life, but they can be challenging to maintain. Whether you want to strengthen your bond with loved ones or repair a strained relationship, the FRMA mantra—focused, rapid, massive action—provides a clear path to building meaningful connections. Relationships thrive on effort, intention, and action, and this chapter will guide you to make them stronger and more fulfilling.

What does FRMA mean for your personal relationships?

Focused action: Understand what matters most

The first step to improving your relationships is gaining clarity.

What do you want to achieve in your connections? Is it better communication, spending more quality time together, or healing past wounds?

Here's how you do it:

- Identify the relationships that need your attention—partner, family, or friends.

- Reflect on what's causing friction or distance. Is it lack of time, unresolved issues, or poor communication?

- Prioritize actions that will have the most significant impact on improving the bond.

Example:

Aarti Verma, a young professional, realized her busy schedule had strained her relationship with her mother. She focused on rebuilding their bond by dedicating weekly time to meaningful conversations. This simple focus reignited their closeness.

Quote:

"The greatest gift you can give someone is your undivided attention."

— **Divya Mehta**

Rapid action: Don't wait to reconnect

When it comes to relationships, the longer you wait, the harder it becomes to bridge the gap. Rapid action is about taking the first step without delay.

Here's how you do it:

- Send a message or make a call to someone you've lost touch with.
- Apologize immediately if you've hurt someone, even if it's uncomfortable.
- Plan small gestures that show your care, like surprising a loved one with something thoughtful.

Example:

Rahul Sharma had drifted apart from his college best friend. He quickly took action by sending a heartfelt message and organizing a catch-up over dinner. Their friendship picked up right where they had left off.

Quote

"Sometimes the smallest step in the right direction ends up being the biggest step of your life."

— **Priyanka Chopra Jonas**

Massive action: Go all in to rebuild or strengthen bonds

For relationships that are deeply strained or have lost trust, small actions alone may not suffice. Massive action is about taking bold, meaningful steps to rebuild or strengthen the connection.

Here's how you do it:

- Plan a trip or significant event to reconnect deeply with a loved one.

- Commit to consistent improvements, such as weekly date nights or regular family dinners.

- Seek professional help, like therapy or counselling, for relationships that need healing.

Example:

Ankit and Meera Singh were on the brink of divorce. As a last attempt, they took massive action by joining a couples therapy program and committing to weekly exercises to improve communication. Today, they credit this bold step for saving their marriage.

Quote:

"Courage is the foundation of all great relationships. It takes bravery to love deeply, forgive completely, and fight for what matters."

Challenges? FRMA has the solutions

1. **"I don't know how to start the conversation."**

   Answer: Start with honesty. A simple "I miss you" or "I'd like to talk" can open the door.

2. **"What if they don't respond?"**

   Answer: Not everyone will react immediately. Stay consistent and give them time.

3. **"The damage feels irreparable."**

   Answer: Massive action, like therapy or a heartfelt gesture, can rebuild even the most broken relationships.

How to implement FRMA

Step 1: Define your focus.

- Be specific. Example: "Reconnect with my brother and rebuild our trust over the next 3 months."

Step 2: Take rapid action.

- Take one immediate step today—send a message, make a call, or apologize.

Step 3: Commit to massive action.

- Plan a significant gesture, like hosting a family reunion, writing a heartfelt letter, or attending counselling.

Practical exercises

1. **Relationship audit**

   - List three relationships you want to improve. For each, write one thing you can do today to make progress.

2. **The gratitude challenge**

   - Write a thank-you note or message to a loved one every day for a week.

3. **The weekly connection plan**

   - Schedule regular time for important people in your life— dinner with your partner, a call with a friend, or a visit to your parents.

Real-life inspiration

Riya Kapoor: Rekindling Family Bonds

Riya had grown distant from her siblings after years of disagreements. She started with focused action, acknowledging their importance in her life. Rapid action followed when she made a surprise visit to her sister's birthday. Her massive action came when she organized a family vacation, which rekindled the closeness they once shared.

Quote:

"It's never too late to say sorry, thank you, or I love you."

– **Riya Kapoor**

Manoj Gupta: Rebuilding a Marriage

Manoj's marriage was on the verge of collapse due to constant work stress. He focused on prioritizing his wife's needs, took rapid action by apologizing and spending quality time, and made a massive gesture—a month-long vacation to reconnect. Today, his marriage is stronger than ever.

Quote

*"Love is a verb, not just a feeling.
Show it through your actions every day."*

– **Manoj Gupta**

Wrap-up: Build the connections you deserve

Relationships need effort, just like any other part of life. With the FRMA mantra, you can bring focus, urgency, and boldness to creating meaningful and lasting bonds. The journey won't always be easy, but every step will bring you closer to the love and connection you seek.

Start today. Take the first step to improving your relationships with focused, rapid, massive action!

Quote to remember:

*"Love and relationships are the most important
investments you will ever make."*

– **Sundar Pichai**

FRMA MANTRA FOR HEALTH TRANSFORMATION

Reclaiming Your Health, Reviving Your Life

Your health is your foundation. Without it, no success feels complete. Whether you want to lose weight, reverse chronic diseases, or regain your energy, the FRMA mantra—focused, rapid, massive action—can be the game-changer in transforming your health. Small steps and bold moves together can lead to incredible results, and this chapter will guide you to take charge of your physical and mental well-being.

What does FRMA mean for your health transformation?

Focused action: Define your health goals clearly

The first step to better health is clarity. What do you want to achieve? Better stamina? Lower blood sugar? Reversal of obesity? Focused action provides the precision needed to direct your efforts and stay on track.

Here's how you do it:

- Identify your top health priority. Is it fitness, weight loss, or disease management?

- Set specific, measurable goals. Example: "Lose 10 kg in 3 months" or "Reduce my fasting sugar to normal levels."

- Commit to a daily routine that supports your health goals.

Example:

Manisha Aggarwal, a 42-year-old diabetic, focused on managing her blood sugar. She started tracking her diet, exercising daily, and avoiding processed foods. In just 6 months, she reversed her diabetes and became a health mentor to others.

Quote:

"Health is not about the weight you lose, but the life you gain."

– Virat Kohli

Rapid action: Start making changes immediately

Don't wait for the perfect day to start. The sooner you take action, the faster you'll see results. Rapid action is about taking the first steps—however small—right now.

Here's how you do it:

- Swap one unhealthy meal with a nutritious one today.

- Begin with 10 minutes of exercise, even if it's a simple walk.

- Book a health check-up or consult a doctor immediately if needed.

Example:

Ravi Mehta, a corporate executive, realized his sedentary lifestyle was harming his health. He took immediate action by joining a gym, cutting out junk food, and adopting mindful eating. Within a year, he lost 20 kg and regained his energy, proving that focused, rapid action can lead to lasting transformation.

Quote:

"Don't wait for tomorrow. Your health transformation starts today."

– Milind Soman, Fitness Icon

Massive action: Make bold moves for lasting change

Massive action is about making transformational decisions that lead to sustainable results. It's about committing fully to your health goals and going beyond half-measures.

Here's how you do it:

- Sign up for a health program, like a marathon training or yoga retreat.

- Invest in a personal trainer, nutritionist, or wellness coach to guide you.

- Commit to a major lifestyle overhaul—quit smoking, go plant-based, or embrace intermittent fasting.

Example:

Arjun Patel was overweight and suffered from sleep apnea. His massive action came when he committed to bariatric surgery and followed a rigorous year-long fitness program. Today, he is 50 kg lighter and regularly runs marathons, demonstrating the power of bold, life-changing decisions.

Quote:

"Transforming your health requires courage to take bold steps."

– Rujuta Diwekar, Celebrity Nutritionist

Challenges? FRMA has the solutions

1. **"I don't have time for exercise."**

   Answer: You don't need hours. Start with 15-20 minutes of movement daily.

2. **"Healthy food is too expensive."**

   Answer: Focus on simple, natural, and home-cooked meals. Healthy doesn't have to mean costly.

3. **"I keep falling off track."**

    Answer: Build accountability. Track your progress and celebrate small wins to stay motivated.

How to implement FRMA

Step 1: Define your focus.

- Write down your goal. Example: "Lose 5 kg in 8 weeks" or "Run 5 km without stopping."

Step 2: Take rapid action.

- Start with small steps today—drink more water, avoid sugary drinks, or take the stairs instead of the elevator.

Step 3: Commit to massive action.

- Make a bold move, like signing up for a fitness challenge, investing in a home gym, or adopting a completely clean diet.

Practical exercises

1. Health journal

- Track your daily food intake, water consumption, exercise, and sleep. This will help you identify patterns and areas for improvement.

2. 30-day challenge

- Pick one habit to adopt for the next 30 days, such as eating home-cooked meals or walking 10,000 steps daily.

3. Vision board

- Create a visual representation of your health goals—photos, quotes, or milestones that inspire you to stay on track.

Real-life inspiration

Sonal Arora: From Obesity to Fitness Icon

Sonal, a 38-year-old mother, weighed 100 kg and struggled with self-esteem. She began with focused action by walking daily. Rapid action followed as she joined a gym and learned portion control. Her massive action was hiring a coach and training for her first 5k run. Today, she's a fitness influencer with a massive online following.

Quote:

"Your body is the only place you have to live. Take care of it."

– Sonal Arora

Ajay Malhotra: Reversing Chronic Illness

Ajay, diagnosed with hypertension, took control of his health with focused meal planning and exercise. His rapid action included cutting out salt-laden processed foods and walking 30 minutes daily. His massive action involved a complete lifestyle transformation, including meditation and strength training. Today, he is medication-free and serves as a health advocate, inspiring others with his transformation.

Quote:

"Your health is an investment, not an expense.
The returns are priceless."

– Ajay Malhotra

Wrap-up: Your health, your responsibility

Your health isn't just about living longer—it's about living better. The FRMA mantra helps you take control with focus, urgency, and boldness. Transforming your health is a journey, but every step brings you closer to a vibrant, energized life.

Take your first step today. Reclaim your health with focused, rapid, massive action!

Quote to remember:

*"It's not about being the best.
It's about being better than you were yesterday."*

– Saina Nehwal, Indian Badminton Champion

FRMA MANTRA FOR RELAUNCHING AFTER A FAILURE

Bounce Back Stronger, Aim Higher

Failure is not the end; it's a reset button. Whether you've faced setbacks in entrepreneurship, exams, career, or relationships, what defines you is how you rise. The FRMA mantra—focused, rapid, massive action—offers a proven roadmap to recover, rebuild, and relaunch yourself. Failure isn't fatal; it's your chance to create a stronger, smarter, and more determined version of yourself.

What does FRMA mean for your comeback?

Focused action: Reassess and redefine your goals

Failure often feels overwhelming, but it's also a powerful opportunity to focus on what truly matters.

Here's how you do it:

- Take time to reflect: What went wrong, and what can you learn from it?
- Redefine your goals to align with your strengths and passions.
- Set clear, actionable priorities to rebuild step by step.

Example:

Ritesh Aggarwal, founder of OYO Rooms, faced early failures when his initial startup failed to gain traction. He focused on the hospitality sector, identified customer pain points, and rebuilt with a laser-sharp strategy. Today, OYO is a global brand.

Quote:

> *"Failure is simply the opportunity to begin again,*
> *this time more intelligently."*

> – Henry Ford

Rapid action: Don't dwell, start acting immediately

The longer you stay stuck in regret, the harder it is to move forward. Rapid action helps you regain momentum and confidence.

Here's how you do it:

- Take one immediate step today: Write down your next goal, send a resume, or reach out for advice.

- Surround yourself with positivity—mentors, friends, or books that inspire action.

- Address small, practical tasks that make you feel productive.

Example:

After failing her first CA attempt, Radhika Sharma immediately identified her weak areas and enrolled in a coaching program. Her quick response paid off—she cleared her CA final on the next attempt.

Quote:

> *"Success is not final, failure is not fatal.*
> *It is the courage to continue that counts."*

> – Winston Churchill

Massive action: Make bold moves to relaunch yourself

True transformation comes from bold, decisive actions. Massive action pushes you beyond your comfort zone, setting the stage for a powerful comeback.

Here's how you do it:

- If you failed in entrepreneurship: Pivot your business model or explore an entirely new market.

- If you failed an exam: Commit to an intensive preparation plan with expert guidance.

- If you faced a career setback: Build a personal brand, network aggressively, or consider upskilling.

Example:

Kailash Katkar, founder of Quick Heal Technologies, went from shutting down his failed repair business to launching a cybersecurity empire. His massive action? Transitioning his expertise into a rapidly growing industry and scaling aggressively.

Quote:

> *"Every setback has the seeds of a comeback.*
> *Plant them, nurture them, and watch yourself grow."*

– Kailash Katkar

Challenges? FRMA has the solutions

1. **"I'm afraid of failing again."**

   Answer: Shift your mindset. Failure is part of the process. Each attempt brings you closer to success.

2. **"I don't know where to start."**

   Answer: Start small. Focus on achievable goals to build momentum and confidence.

3. **"I feel judged by others."**

   Answer: Let your results do the talking. Ignore negativity and focus on your growth.

How to implement FRMA

Step 1: Define your focus.

- Identify one clear goal for your relaunch. Example: "Secure a leadership role in marketing within 6 months" or "Rebuild my startup with a new target audience."

Step 2: Take rapid action.

- Take the first step today—whether it's researching opportunities, applying for jobs, or creating a revised business plan.

Step 3: Commit to massive action.

- Make bold moves, like pitching to investors, enrolling in an advanced course, or partnering with industry leaders.

Practical exercises

1. Post-failure audit

- Write down what went wrong, what you learned, and how you'll avoid repeating those mistakes.

2. The 30-day momentum challenge

- Commit to taking one action every day for 30 days that aligns with your comeback goal.

3. The bold move tracker

- Identify and execute one significant action every week, like networking with influential people or launching a pilot project.

Real-life inspiration

Kiran Mazumdar-Shaw: From Rejection to Biocon Founder

Kiran faced rejection when her first brewing job application was turned down due to gender bias. She refocused her energy on entrepreneurship and took massive action by starting Biocon in her garage. Today, she's one of the most respected business leaders in India.

Quote:

"My ideas were questioned. My abilities were doubted. But I never let rejection define me."

– **Kiran Mazumdar-Shaw**

Ankit Agarwal: From Startup Failure to Success

After his first startup failed, Ankit pivoted to creating an eco-friendly product line. His massive action included scaling his brand's presence at global trade shows. Today, his company, Phool. co, is a global success story.

Quote:

"Failure is not a wall; it's a door to a better opportunity."

– **Ankit Agarwal**

Wrap-up: Your comeback story starts here

Failure is a chapter, not your whole story. The FRMA mantra helps you focus on your strengths, take immediate action, and make bold moves to relaunch yourself. Every great achiever has faced setbacks—what sets them apart is their resilience and determination to bounce back.

Quote to remember:

"Success is how high you bounce after you hit rock bottom." — General George S. Patton

Your comeback is waiting. Take the first step today with focused, rapid, massive action!

FRMA MANTRA FOR PEOPLE AT A CROSSROADS

Clarity, Courage, and the Power of Timely Decisions

Life is full of crossroads, moments when you face multiple options and struggle to decide the right path. Whether it's choosing a career, starting a business, or making a life-changing decision, hesitation and procrastination can hold you back. The FRMA mantra—focused, rapid, massive action—empowers you to break through indecision, find clarity, and act decisively to seize the best opportunities.

What does FRMA mean for you at a crossroads?

Focused action: Define your priorities

The first step is to quiet the noise. When faced with too many choices, clarity is your greatest ally. Focused action helps you zero in on what truly matters.

Here's how you do it:

- Write down your goals. What is your ultimate priority—financial growth, personal fulfilment, or family stability?
- Analyze each option against your goals. Which aligns most with your long-term vision?
- Eliminate distractions and stop overanalyzing less important choices.

Example:

Priya Mehta, an MBA graduate, was torn between a high-paying corporate job and starting her own social enterprise. By focusing on her passion for creating impact, she chose entrepreneurship.

Her clarity led to the launch of a successful nonprofit that's now helping thousands of women.

Quote:

"Decisions become easier when your vision is clear."

– **Ratan Tata**

Rapid action: Act before the opportunity slips away

The longer you wait, the more opportunities you miss. Rapid action is about making timely decisions and taking the first steps to implement them.

Here's how you do it:

- Set a deadline for your decision. Commit to acting within days, not weeks.

- Start with a small step that moves you closer to your chosen path—research, network, or test your idea.

- Trust your instincts once you've weighed the pros and cons.

Example:

Rahul Gupta, a young engineer, couldn't decide between moving abroad for a stable job or staying in India to work at a startup. He acted quickly, accepting the startup offer and building his skills. This rapid decision fast-tracked his career into leadership roles.

Quote:

"Indecision is the thief of opportunity. Take action before it's too late."

– **Dhirubhai Ambani**

Massive action: Commit boldly to your choice

Once you've decided, go all in. Massive action transforms hesitation into momentum and ensures you make the most of your decision.

Here's how you do it:

- **Set a bold goal** aligned with your choice and commit to achieving it.
- **Invest your time, energy, and resources** wholeheartedly in your goal.
- **Stay consistent** and avoid second-guessing your decision.

Example:

Shalini Sharma, a mid-career professional, chose to switch industries despite the risks. Her massive action involved taking certification courses, networking aggressively, and applying to roles outside her comfort zone. Within a year, she transitioned successfully into her dream role in sustainability.

Quote:

"Once you make a decision, the universe conspires to make it happen."

– Paulo Coelho

Challenges? FRMA has the solutions

1. **"I'm afraid of making the wrong decision."**

   Answer: There's no perfect choice. Focus on what aligns best with your values and act confidently.

2. **"What if I regret my choice?"**

   Answer: Every decision teaches you something valuable. Growth comes from action, not inaction.

3. **"I feel overwhelmed by too many options."**

   Answer: Narrow it down to 2-3 options and weigh them against your top priorities.

How to implement FRMA

Step 1: Define your focus.

- Clarify what you want to achieve. Example: "Start my own business within 6 months" or "Move to a new role in tech."

Step 2: Take rapid action.

- Commit to a decision within a set timeframe, like 48 hours. Take the first step immediately, whether it's applying for a job, building a prototype, or seeking mentorship.

Step 3: Commit to massive action.

- Set a bold, measurable target and work consistently to achieve it.

Practical exercises

1. **Decision clarity worksheet**

   - List your options, pros, and cons. Choose the one that aligns most with your long-term goals.

2. **The 48-hour decision rule**

   - Give yourself 48 hours to make a decision and act on it.

3. **The all-in commitment tracker**

   - Write down your chosen goal and track daily actions to stay on course.

Real-life inspiration

Kavita Joshi: From Confusion to CEO

Kavita was at a crossroads, unsure whether to expand her small business or take a corporate leadership role. She focused on her passion for entrepreneurship, acted quickly by seeking expert advice, and made a bold move to scale her business internationally.

Today, she leads a multimillion-dollar company, proving the power of decisive action.

Quote:

"Success is about making bold decisions and standing by them."

– Kavita Joshi

Amit Sinha: Choosing Growth Over Comfort

Amit, an IT professional, was torn between staying in his secure job and pursuing an MBA abroad. He rapidly decided to invest in his education and took massive action by securing a scholarship. This decision opened doors to global opportunities, transforming his career trajectory.

Quote:

"Every great achievement starts with the courage to make a choice."

– Amit Sinha

Wrap-up: Choose your path with confidence

Standing at a crossroads can feel paralyzing, but it's also an opportunity to shape your future. The FRMA mantra gives you the clarity, urgency, and boldness to make decisions that matter. Don't let indecision hold you back. Trust yourself, take action, and commit fully to your chosen path.

Quote to remember:

"The best way to predict the future is to create it."

– Peter Drucker

Start now. The road to your future is yours to choose—focus, act, and transform your crossroads into success with the FRMA mantra!

4. Appendices or Tools

Appendix: Practical Tools for Implementing FRMA

To help you apply the principles of **Focused, Rapid, Massive Action** in your life, here are a few practical tools and worksheets you can use right away:

1. **FRMA Action Plan Template**
   Define your goals and outline the specific actions you will take to achieve them. This template will help you break down your vision into clear, actionable steps.

2. **Daily Focus Tracker**
   Use this tracker to maintain daily focus on your high-impact actions. Write down your key tasks for the day and review your progress at the end of each day.

3. **SMART Goals Worksheet**
   Create clear and measurable goals by using the SMART criteria (Specific, Measurable, Achievable, Relevant, and Time-bound). This worksheet will guide you in setting goals that are aligned with your vision.

4. **Massive Action Checklist**
   Identify one bold, massive action you can take to accelerate your progress and track your steps to completion.

5. **Weekly Progress Review**
   Reflect on your progress at the end of each week. What did you accomplish? What challenges did you face? How can you adjust your actions to stay aligned with your goals?

FRMA Action Plan Template

1. Define Your Vision:

What do you want to achieve in the next 12 months?

- **Vision Statement:**
  (Example: "I want to grow my business by 50% and secure three high-profile clients.")

2. Identify High-Impact Actions:

What are the top 3 actions you can take that will move you closer to your vision?

6. **Action 1:**
   (Example: "Develop a new marketing campaign focused on a specific target audience.")

7. **Action 2:**
   (Example: "Build partnerships with industry influencers to enhance credibility.")

8. **Action 3:**
   (Example: "Launch a referral program to encourage word-of-mouth growth.")

3. Set 24-Hour Action Deadline:

What is one small step you can take in the next 24 hours to begin executing each of your high-impact actions?

1. **Action 1 First Step (Next 24 Hours):**
   (Example: "Schedule a meeting with the marketing team to brainstorm campaign ideas.")

2. **Action 2 First Step (Next 24 Hours):**
   (Example: "Reach out to two potential industry influencers for collaboration.")

3. **Action 3 First Step (Next 24 Hours):**
   (Example: "Draft a proposal for the referral program and discuss it with the team.")

4. Plan Your Massive Action:

What bold, massive action can you take within the next 7 days to accelerate your progress toward your vision?

- **Massive** **Action:**
  (Example: "Host a live webinar to introduce the company to a new audience and offer exclusive deals.")

5. Track Your Progress:

Use a daily or weekly tracker to monitor your progress on the actions outlined above. Make note of any adjustments you need to make to stay aligned with your vision.

4. **Review Date:**
   (Example: Weekly progress review every Friday.)

5. **Adjustments Needed:**
   (Example: "Modify the referral program based on feedback from initial clients.")

6. Reflect and Adjust:

At the end of each week, ask yourself:

- What did I accomplish?

- What challenges did I face?

- What actions do I need to adjust or prioritize for the upcoming week?

This template is designed to help you focus on the most impactful actions, act swiftly, and take bold steps to achieve your goals. Stay committed, and make continuous progress with this structured plan!

Daily Focus Tracker

Date: [Insert Date]

1. Top 3 High-Impact Actions for Today:

- **Action 1:**
  (Example: "Complete draft of the new marketing campaign.")

- **Action 2:**
  (Example: "Follow up with 3 potential clients for partnerships.")

- **Action 3:**
  (Example: "Analyze performance metrics for the past quarter.")

2. Key Tasks for Each Action:

Action 1 Tasks:

- Task 1:
  (Example: "Research key trends for the campaign.")
- Task 2:
  (Example: "Write content for campaign materials.")
- Task 3:
  (Example: "Send draft to marketing team for feedback.")

Action 2 Tasks:

- Task 1:
  (Example: "Call potential client A.")
- Task 2:
  (Example: "Email follow-up proposal to client B.")
- Task 3:
  (Example: "Schedule meeting with client C.")

Action 3 Tasks:

- Task 1:
  (Example: "Compile sales data for last 3 months.")
- Task 2:
  (Example: "Analyze customer engagement trends.")
- Task 3:
  (Example: "Summarize findings for tomorrow's meeting.")

3. Progress Reflection:

- **What went well today?**
  (Example: "Completed draft of the campaign and got valuable feedback.")

- **What challenges did you face?**
  (*Example: "Delayed response from potential clients, need to follow up again."*)

- **What can you improve for tomorrow?**
  (*Example: "Prioritize client follow-ups earlier in the day."*)

4. Adjustments for Tomorrow:

- **Carryover tasks from today (if any):**
  (*Example: "Follow-up with client C."*)

- **New focus areas for tomorrow:**
  (*Example: "Start reviewing metrics for the new product launch."*)

5. End-of-Day Rating:

- **How focused and productive were you today?**
  (*Rate yourself on a scale of 1-10 and provide a brief reflection on your performance.*)
  Rating: ___
  Reflection: (*Example: "Overall, productive but could improve follow-up efforts with clients."*)

This **Daily Focus Tracker** is designed to keep you on track, ensuring that you make steady progress on your high-impact actions each day. It promotes accountability and reflection, enabling you to adjust your approach for continuous improvement.

SMART Goals Worksheet

Goal Title:

(Example: "Increase Sales by 20% in Q4")

1. Specific

- **What exactly do you want to achieve?**
  (*Describe the goal clearly and in detail.*)

(*Example: "Increase our sales revenue by 20% in the next quarter through targeted marketing campaigns and partnerships."*)

- **Why is this goal important?**
  (*Explain the reason behind this goal.*)
  (*Example: "To boost company profitability and reach our year-end revenue targets."*)

- **Who is involved?**
  (*Identify the people, teams, or resources needed to achieve this goal.*)
  (*Example: "Sales team, marketing team, and external partners."*)

2. Measurable

- How will you measure progress and success?
  (*Identify the specific metrics or key performance indicators (KPIs) that will track progress.*)
  (*Example: "Track the sales numbers weekly, monitor conversion rates, and measure the success of each marketing campaign."*)

- What is the target outcome?
  (*Example: "Achieve $500,000 in sales revenue by the end of the quarter."*)

3. Achievable

- **Is the goal realistic and attainable?**
  (*Assess whether the goal is challenging yet achievable given available resources, time, and skills.*)
  (*Example: "Based on past performance and upcoming product launches, a 20% increase is realistic with the right focus and effort."*)

- **What steps will you take to achieve this goal?**
  (*Break down the goal into smaller tasks or milestones.*)

☐ **Step 1:** *(Example: "Launch two new targeted marketing campaigns within the first month.")*

☐ **Step 2:** *(Example: "Train sales team on upselling strategies by mid-quarter.")*

☐ **Step 3:** *(Example: "Host a partnership event to attract new clients by the end of the second month.")*

4. Relevant

- **Why does this goal align with your broader business or personal objectives?**
  (Explain how the goal fits within your overall strategy or mission.)
  (Example: "This sales goal supports our larger objective of increasing market share and meeting our yearly revenue targets.")

- **How will achieving this goal impact the organization or your personal growth?**
  (Example: "It will improve profitability, enhance brand reputation, and strengthen our team's capabilities in sales and marketing.")

5. Time-bound

- **What is the deadline for achieving this goal?**
  (Set a clear and realistic deadline for the completion of the goal.)
  (Example: "December 31st, 2024.")

- **What are the key milestones along the way?**

  ☐ **Milestone 1:** *(Example: "Achieve a 5% increase in sales by the end of the first month.")*

  ☐ **Milestone 2:** *(Example: "Reach a 10% increase in sales by the end of the second month.")*

  ☐ **Milestone 3:** *(Example: "Hit the full 20% increase by the end of the quarter.")*

Summary of Your SMART Goal

- **Goal:** *(Example: "Increase sales revenue by 20% in Q4 through targeted marketing and improved sales strategies.")*

- **Measurement:** *(Example: "Track sales growth weekly and measure marketing campaign effectiveness.")*

- **Achievability:** *(Example: "Based on past results, the goal is realistic and achievable with the current resources.")*

- **Relevance:** *(Example: "Supports broader business objectives of growing market share.")*

- **Time-bound:** *(Example: "Complete the goal by December 31st, 2024, with key milestones along the way.")*

By filling out this **SMART Goals Worksheet**, you'll have a clear, structured plan that will guide your efforts and ensure your goals are Specific, Measurable, Achievable, Relevant, and Time-bound.

Massive Action Checklist

1. Define Your Massive Action

- **What is the one bold, massive action you can take to accelerate your progress?**
  (Describe the big step you are committing to taking.)
  (Example: "Launch a new product line in three months to target a new market segment.")

- **Why is this action crucial for your success?**
  (Explain why this massive action is essential to achieving your larger goals.)
  (Example: "This will allow us to expand into a growing market and increase revenue by 30% over the next year.")

2. Break It Down into Smaller Steps

- What are the key tasks required to accomplish this massive action?

☐ **Task 1:** *(Example: "Conduct market research and finalize the product concept within 2 weeks.")*

☐ **Task 2:** *(Example: "Develop the product prototype in the next 30 days.")*

☐ **Task 3:** *(Example: "Secure manufacturing and supply chain partners in the next 45 days.")*

☐ **Task 4:** *(Example: "Launch marketing campaign 60 days before product release.")*

☐ **Task 5:** *(Example: "Execute the product launch event in three months.")*

3. Set a Deadline for Completion

- **What is the exact deadline for completing your massive action?**
  (Set a clear and specific date for achieving this bold step.)
  (Example: "Product launch date: March 31st, 2025.")

- **Are there intermediate milestones along the way?**

  ☐ **Milestone 1:** *(Example: "Prototype ready by February 1st, 2025.")*

  ☐ **Milestone 2:** *(Example: "Marketing campaign launched by February 15th, 2025.")*

  ☐ **Milestone 3:** *(Example: "Final product ready for manufacturing by March 1st, 2025.")*

4. Identify Potential Challenges

- **What obstacles or risks might you encounter?**
  (List potential challenges you may face while executing this massive action.)
  (Example: "Potential delays in product development, manufacturing issues, or budget constraints.")

- **How will you mitigate these challenges?**
  (Outline solutions or contingency plans for each identified risk.)
  (Example: "Create a backup plan with alternative suppliers,

monitor budget closely, and build buffer time into the timeline.")*

5. Assemble Resources and Support

- **What resources, tools, or people do you need to accomplish this massive action?**
  (Identify the key resources and support required to execute your plan.)
  (Example: "Marketing team, product developers, manufacturing partners, and a dedicated project manager.")

- **Who can hold you accountable for taking action?**
  (List any accountability partners, mentors, or colleagues who will help you stay on track.)
  (Example: "Assign a project manager to track progress and report weekly updates.")

6. Take the First Step

- **What is the very first action you can take right now?**
  (Identify the first immediate step to get started on your massive action.)
  (Example: "Schedule a team meeting to finalize the product concept.")

- **Set a deadline for completing this first step:**
  (Example: "Complete this first step within 24 hours.")

7. Track Your Progress

- **How will you track the progress of your massive action?**
  (Choose a method to monitor your progress, such as a weekly review, project management tools, or regular check-ins.)
  (Example: "Use a project management tool to track milestones and progress, with weekly team updates.")

8. Celebrate Milestones and Achievements

- **How will you celebrate each milestone?**
  (Acknowledge progress along the way to maintain motivation.)

(Example: "Celebrate the completion of the prototype with a team lunch or recognition event.")

✦✦✦

Summary of Your Massive Action

- **Massive Action:** *(Example: "Launch a new product line to enter a new market.")*

- **Deadline:** *(Example: "March 31st, 2025.")*

- **Key Steps:** *(Example: "Develop prototype, secure suppliers, launch marketing, execute product launch.")*

- **Challenges:** *(Example: "Potential development delays, budget constraints.")*

- **First Step:** *(Example: "Schedule team meeting within 24 hours.")*

By using this **Massive Action Checklist**, you'll be able to turn bold ideas into concrete actions that accelerate your progress toward your most important goals.

✦✦✦

Weekly Progress Review

1. Review Your Goals for the Week

- **What were your primary goals for the week?**
  (List the main objectives or targets you set at the start of the week.)
  (Example: "Complete the first draft of the project proposal, finalize new client agreements, and conduct team training.")

- **Did you achieve these goals? Why or why not?**

  - ☐ **Goal 1:** *(Example: "Project proposal completed.")*

  - ☐ **Goal 2:** *(Example: "Client agreements finalized.")*

  - ☐ **Goal 3:** *(Example: "Team training postponed due to scheduling conflicts.")*

2. Assess Your High-Impact Actions

- **What high-impact actions did you focus on this week?**
  (List the actions that were most important for achieving your goals.)
  (Example: "Held client meetings, delegated tasks to the team, and prepared the project outline.")

- **Were these actions effective?**
  (Evaluate whether these actions brought you closer to achieving your weekly objectives.)
  (Example: "Client meetings were successful, but the project outline needs more refinement.")

3. Identify Wins and Accomplishments

- **What were your biggest wins this week?**
  (Highlight key achievements or breakthroughs, no matter how small.)
  (Example: "Secured two new client contracts, completed 80% of the project proposal.")

- **What contributed to these successes?**
  (Identify factors such as focus, teamwork, or rapid decision-making that helped you achieve these wins.)
  (Example: "Proactive communication with clients and efficient task delegation.")

4. Reflect on Challenges and Obstacles

- **What challenges or obstacles did you encounter this week?**
  (List any difficulties or setbacks that hindered your progress.)
  (Example: "Unexpected delays in team coordination, missed deadlines, or external factors.")

- **How did you handle these challenges?**
  (Evaluate how effectively you responded to the obstacles.)
  (Example: "Rescheduled meetings and streamlined communication channels to address team delays.")

- **What could you improve moving forward?**
  (Think about what you could do differently to overcome these challenges next time.)
  (Example: "Improve time management and set clearer deadlines for team tasks.")

5. Adjustments and Course Corrections

- **What adjustments do you need to make to stay on track?**
  (Identify any changes you need to implement in your strategy, actions, or focus.)
  (Example: "Shift more time toward finalizing the project proposal and prioritize team alignment next week.")

- **Are your current goals still aligned with your long-term vision?**
  (Check if your weekly goals are contributing to your overall success and vision.)
  (Example: "Yes, the proposal is critical to securing long-term projects and growth.")

6. Plan for the Next Week

- **What are your top 3 priorities for the upcoming week?**
  (Set clear objectives for the next week to stay focused and productive.)

  - ☐ **Priority 1:** *(Example: "Finalize the project proposal and submit to clients.")*

  - ☐ **Priority 2:** *(Example: "Conduct rescheduled team training.")*

  - ☐ **Priority 3:** *(Example: "Initiate marketing campaign for new product launch.")*

- **What high-impact actions will you take to achieve these priorities?**
  (List the key actions you'll focus on to accomplish your goals next week.)
  (Example: "Review project proposal daily, schedule client follow-ups, prepare team training materials.")

7. Celebrate and Acknowledge Progress

- **How will you celebrate your wins from this week?**
  (*Recognize your efforts and celebrate the progress you've made, no matter how small.*)
  (*Example: "Treat myself to a nice dinner or take a relaxing day off."*)

- **Who can you acknowledge for their contributions to your progress?**
  (*Express appreciation for team members, colleagues, or mentors who supported your success.*)
  (*Example: "Thank my team for their hard work on the client agreements and project support."*)

Summary of Your Weekly Review

- **Biggest Wins:** (*Example: "Secured two client contracts, completed most of the project proposal."*)

- **Challenges:** (*Example: "Team delays and missed deadlines."*)

- **Adjustments Needed:** (*Example: "Focus on time management and team coordination."*)

- **Top Priorities for Next Week:** (*Example: "Finalize proposal, team training, marketing campaign."*)

By conducting this **Weekly Progress Review**, you'll stay aligned with your goals, celebrate your successes, and make the necessary adjustments to keep moving forward toward your long-term vision.

5. Suggested Reading

Suggested Reading

To further your journey toward success and personal transformation, here are a few books and resources that have inspired and informed the concepts shared in this book:

1. **The 7 Habits of Highly Effective People** by Stephen Covey
    A timeless classic that explores the habits of successful people and how they prioritize, focus, and take action.

2. **Atomic Habits** by James Clear
    A practical guide to building good habits and breaking bad ones. Clear offers actionable strategies for making small changes that lead to significant results over time.

3. **The Power of Now** by Eckhart Tolle
    A powerful exploration of the importance of being present and taking action in the current moment.

4. **Awaken the Giant Within** by Tony Robbins
    Tony Robbins' book on personal development, offers strategies for taking control of your emotions, your finances, your relationships, and your life.

5. **The Lean Startup** by Eric Ries
    A guide to rapid iteration and innovation for entrepreneurs, emphasizing the importance of acting quickly and learning from real-world feedback.